Eyewitness
CHEMISTRY

Model of the molecular structure of tartaric acid (1914)

Silica gel is used in a desiccator to remove moisture

A precipitation reaction where potassium iodide is added to lead nitrate

Kipps apparatus for the preparation of hydrogen sulfide

Early 20th-century view of what an atom looks like

Saffron and turmeric, used to color foods and fabrics since ancient times

Precipitates of substances with hydrogen sulfide

The acid in a bee sting can be soothed by alkaline ointment

Bromine: one of the nonmetal elements

Eyewitness
CHEMISTRY

Written by
Dr. ANN NEWMARK

The molecules in citrus fruits contribute to their odor

Potassium permangenate dissolving in water

Two metal salts derived from the element copper

Egyptian mummified cat

DK Publishing, Inc.

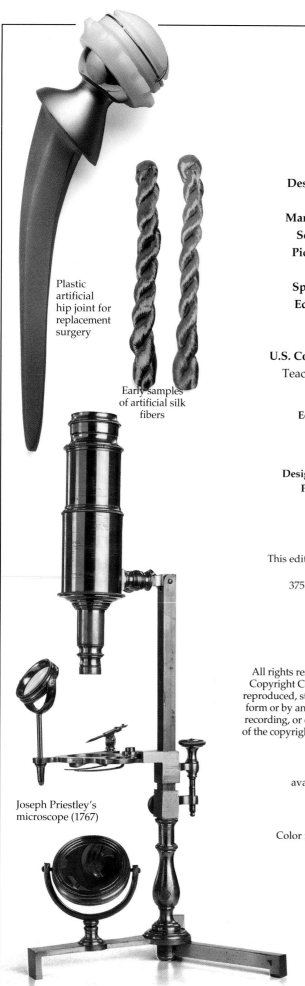

Plastic artificial hip joint for replacement surgery

Early samples of artificial silk fibers

Joseph Priestley's microscope (1767)

DK

LONDON, NEW YORK, MUNICH,
MELBOURNE, and DELHI

Project Editor Charyn Jones
Art Editor Heather McCarry
Designer Marianna Papachrysanthou
Production Louise Daly
Managing Editor Josephine Buchanan
Senior Art Editor Thomas Keenes
Picture Research Deborah Pownall,
Catherine O'Rourke
Special Photography Clive Streeter
Editorial Consultant Peter Morris,
Science Museum, London
U.S. Editor Charles A. Wills
U.S. Consultant Professor Peter W. Morgan,
Teachers College, Columbia University

REVISED EDITION
Editors Barbara Berger, Laura Buller
Editorial assistant John Searcy
Publishing director Beth Sutinis
Senior designer Tai Blanche
Designers Jessica Lasher, Diana Catherines
Phototo research Chrissy McIntyre
Art director Dirk Kaufman
DTP designer Milos Orlovic
Production Ivor Parker

This edition published in the United States in 2005
by DK Publishing, Inc.
375 Hudson Street, New York, NY 10014

13 14 12 11 10 9 8
009-ED369-Sept/2005

A catalog record for this book is
available from the Library of Congress.

ISBN-13: 978-0-7566-1385-3 (plc)
ISBN-13: 978-0-7566-1394-5 (alb)

Color reproduction by Colourscan, Singapore
Printed and bound in China by
South China Printing Co. Ltd

Discover more at
www.dk.com

Simplified model of deoxyribonucleic acid (DNA)

Glass eudiometer for measuring the purity of air (c. 1820)

Contents

A displacement reaction in which copper displaces silver from a solution of silver salts

What is chemistry?

CHEMISTRY IS THE SCIENCE OF CHANGE. It looks at all the different kinds of substances and how they interact with each other. It is going on all around us all the time (pp. 8-9), as well as in the scientific laboratory and in the chemical industry. People in widely differing walks of life use chemistry everyday – the doctor and the chef, the farmer and the builder. Chemistry comes to the aid of the manufacturer of food, and also to the brewer and wine maker. The technician in the hospital laboratory uses chemistry to check for infections in blood samples (pp. 60-61). The forensic scientist uses chemistry to solve crimes (pp. 42-43). In agriculture, chemistry is used to increase the yield of crops and to control many pests (pp. 62-63). Chemicals keep the water supply safe and swimming pools clean. One of the largest industries in the world is the petrochemical industry – this industry is mainly associated with gasoline and the chemicals that come from crude oil (pp. 62-63). Drugs, synthetic dyes, plastics, and fabrics are produced by chemical means from Nature's raw materials.

PLASTER CAST
Gypsum is a form of calcium sulfate that contains some water in its structure. Heating it removes 75 percent of the water, producing powdered plaster of Paris, used here to correct a deformity of the spine.

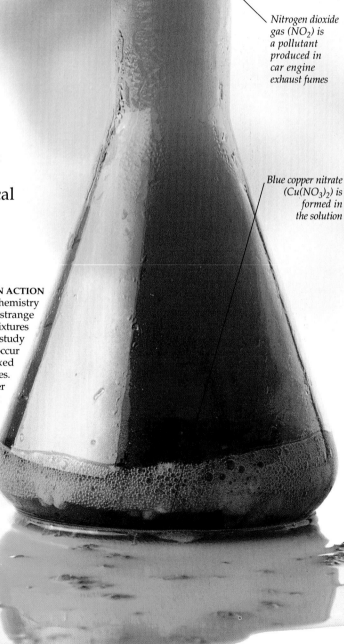

Nitrogen dioxide gas (NO_2) is a pollutant produced in car engine exhaust fumes

Blue copper nitrate ($Cu(NO_3)_2$) is formed in the solution

CHEMISTRY IN ACTION
The popular view of chemistry is one with test tubes, strange smells, and evil-looking mixtures in the laboratory. Chemists study the chemical reactions that occur when substances are mixed together to form new substances. Here nitric acid is added to copper metal. The brown gas (the pollutant nitrogen dioxide) is produced so quickly that it makes the liquid fizz up and spill. To describe chemical reactions, chemists have developed a language, using internationally recognized symbols and equations. This reaction can be written as:

$$Cu + 4HNO_3 \rightarrow Cu(NO_3)_2 + 2NO_2 + 2H_2O$$

ACID RAIN FOREST
These spruce trees in Poland have been badly damaged by acid rain. This is caused by gases such as sulfur dioxide, which are emitted from factories. When these gases react with moisture in the atmosphere, they form dilute acids. The prevailing wind can carry this pollution some distance before releasing it in rainfall that damages vegetation and lakes.

Water (H_2O) is also produced in the reaction

CHEMICALS AS DETECTOR
Alcohol is absorbed into the blood. From there it is passed to the air that is breathed out. This blow-in-the-bag breathalyzer contains a yellow chemical in the mouthpiece that turns green when it reacts with alcohol in the breath. This allows the police to check for levels of alcohol in the blood of a driver who may have been driving dangerously.

Plastic bag is filled with air from lungs

Nozzle

Yellow crystals

Steel container

Mouthpiece

Bottle containing sulfuric acid – bottle is broken by stopper when container is inverted

Lead stopper

Solution of sodium hydrogencarbonate in cylinder

The acid reacts with sodium hydrogencarbonate to produce carbon dioxide gas

Tap for draining off residue

SODA ACID EXTINGUISHER
A chemical reaction makes a water solution shoot out of the nozzle of this fire extinguisher. The two reacting substances – an acid and a base (pp. 42-43) – are kept apart until the extinguisher is needed. When they are mixed together, carbon dioxide gas is produced, which forces the water out of the cylinder.

Door to furnace

FOOD SUBSTITUTES
Chemistry is widely used in the food industry to manufacture new convenient foodstuffs and to check for impurities (pp. 60-61). Butter is known as a saturated fat, whereas most vegetable oils, which are normally liquid, are polyunsaturated fats. They can be changed to solids, such as margarine, by a chemical process called hydrogenation – the addition of hydrogen to the oils using a catalyst (pp. 36-37), such as nickel. Hydrogenation makes the oil more like butter and easier to spread. Margarine was first developed in the 1860s in France as a cheap butter substitute.

AN ANCIENT PRACTICE
Distillation is an ancient art. It is a method of separating a mixture (pp. 14-15) by boiling and condensing. The distiller could prepare spirits, known as *aqua ardens* (burning water) or *aqua vitae* (water of life), from alcohol obtained by fermentation. Essential oils for medical use could also be prepared this way.

Valve

Model of pot still

Vapor rises up through neck

Copper still where mixture is heated

Delivery tube

Copper coils in which vapor is condensed

DISTILLING MIXTURES
Many different types of still were developed to distill mixtures. When the mixture is heated, substances with the lowest boiling points evaporate first. The vapor containing a greater proportion of alcohol is then cooled in a condenser and the residue is left behind. Malt whisky, first produced in the 16th century, is distilled from an alcohol mixture obtained by fermenting barley and water.

Brick surround

Wooden cooling vat

PHYSICAL OR CHEMICAL?
Not all changes are chemical. When ice melts to form water, or water boils to form steam, no chemical reaction takes place, but the physical state changes. The behavior of the individual units (molecules, pp. 16-17) of the water is different in each case. The attractions between the molecules form a rigid structure in a solid. As the molecules slide over each other, the structure is less rigid in the liquid. Heating causes the molecules to dart around and bump into each other in a gas.

Solid

Liquid

Gas

Molecules form a rigid structure

Molecules slide over each other

Molecules are widely spaced

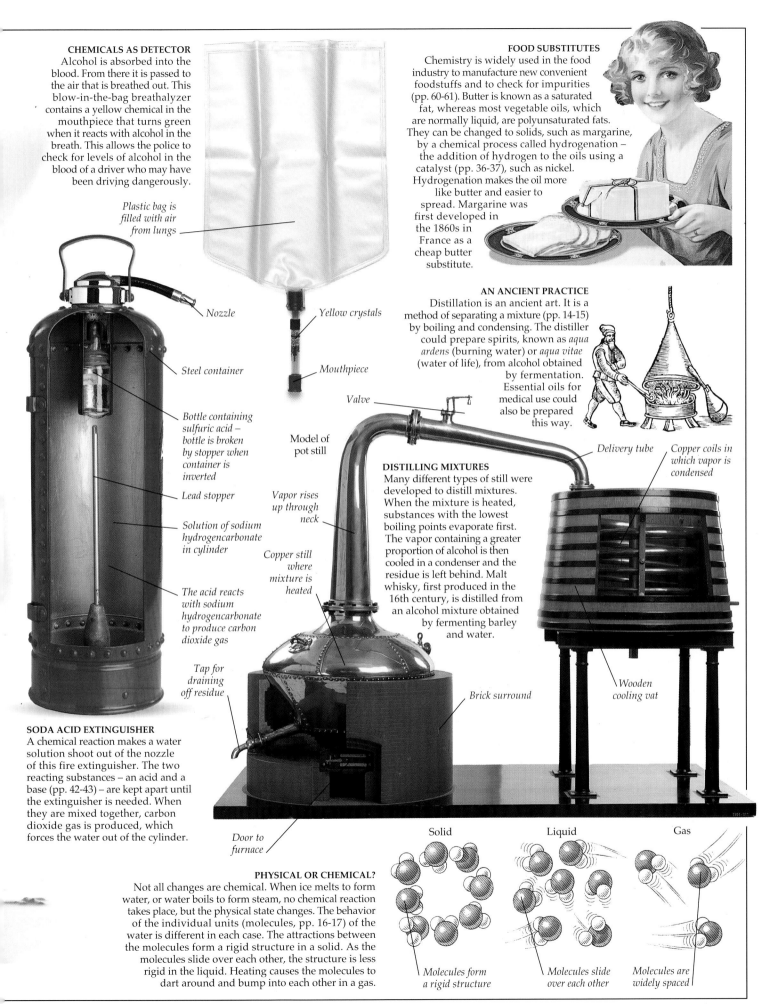

Chemistry in nature

CHEMICAL CHANGE HAS ALWAYS BEEN part of the Universe, even before human beings evolved. Indeed, scientists believe that life began on Earth as a result of complex chemicals reproducing themselves over billions of years. Chemistry is a physial science; it lies between the biological sciences, helping to explain many of life's processes (pp. 50-51), and the laws of physics, which include matter and energy. Chemical processes are constantly occurring within us – when our bodies move, a series of chemical reactions takes place to give the muscles the energy that is taken in from food. Many species of the animal world make use of chemistry to defend themselves, to kill their prey, and to build fragile structures that have incredible strength. Modern methods of chemical analysis have led to a greater understanding of the chemistry of nature, so that it is possible to identify those chemical compounds (pp. 20-21) that produce the color, taste, and smell of a flower or a fruit.

STRONGER THAN STEEL
This garden spider makes its web from fine, silk threads of protein. Amazingly, this thread of protein is stronger than a thread of similar thickness made of steel. The spider can even vary the thread – firm, dry threads for the spokes, and sticky threads to capture prey.

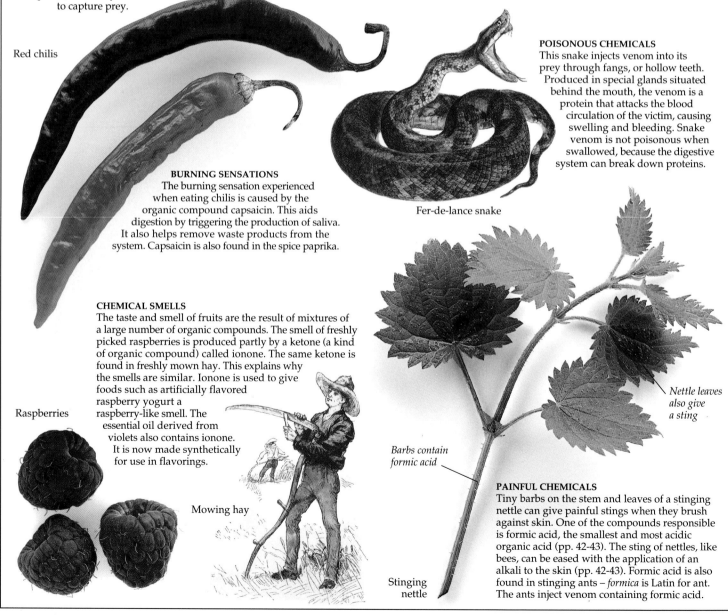

Red chilis

BURNING SENSATIONS
The burning sensation experienced when eating chilis is caused by the organic compound capsaicin. This aids digestion by triggering the production of saliva. It also helps remove waste products from the system. Capsaicin is also found in the spice paprika.

POISONOUS CHEMICALS
This snake injects venom into its prey through fangs, or hollow teeth. Produced in special glands situated behind the mouth, the venom is a protein that attacks the blood circulation of the victim, causing swelling and bleeding. Snake venom is not poisonous when swallowed, because the digestive system can break down proteins.

Fer-de-lance snake

CHEMICAL SMELLS
The taste and smell of fruits are the result of mixtures of a large number of organic compounds. The smell of freshly picked raspberries is produced partly by a ketone (a kind of organic compound) called ionone. The same ketone is found in freshly mown hay. This explains why the smells are similar. Ionone is used to give foods such as artificially flavored raspberry yogurt a raspberry-like smell. The essential oil derived from violets also contains ionone. It is now made synthetically for use in flavorings.

Raspberries

Mowing hay

Nettle leaves also give a sting

Barbs contain formic acid

PAINFUL CHEMICALS
Tiny barbs on the stem and leaves of a stinging nettle can give painful stings when they brush against skin. One of the compounds responsible is formic acid, the smallest and most acidic organic acid (pp. 42-43). The sting of nettles, like bees, can be eased with the application of an alkali to the skin (pp. 42-43). Formic acid is also found in stinging ants – *formica* is Latin for ant. The ants inject venom containing formic acid.

Stinging nettle

UNDERGROUND LIMESTONE DEPOSITS
Limestone rocks consist mainly of calcium carbonate
derived from the shells and skeletons of species such
as shellfish. As rainwater percolates through rocks, it
dissolves small amounts of the calcium carbonate.
Where underground caverns have been formed, the
water drips through the roof, and some evaporates,
depositing solid carbonate on the roof. Over
thousands of years, the deposit grows into a stalactite,
like these in caverns in Florida.

DIGESTIVE PROCESS
Escherichia coli (or *E. coli* for short) are
bacteria that inhabit our intestines.
They are able to break down some of the
foods we eat, such as green vegetables
and beans, into different nutrients.
In the chemical process, gases
are released, which is the
reason for flatulence after a
meal of legumes. *E. coli* also
make vitamin K, which is
needed to make blood clot.
They cause disease only if they
get into the bloodstream; in the
intestine, they are harmless.

*Melanin changes in the
skin mimic the colors
of the branch*

*Peel contains
essential oils*

CHEMICAL CAMOUFLAGE
The chameleon, like the octopus, squid,
and cuttlefish, can alter the color of its
skin to disguise itself from prey. The
compound chiefly responsible is
melanin, which also helps the human
skin tan in the sun. The chameleon's
melanin-producing cells can be activated
by fear or anger; they disperse melanin
granules to produce colors ranging
from yellow to brown and black,
masking the chameleon's normal
coloring. When the melanin comes
together again, the color returns to
the original green. Some chameleons
are able to change their skin color
to blue and bright red.

*Carotene
provides the
orange color*

*Citric acid from lemons is
used to flavor lemonade*

ORANGES AND LEMONS
The odor of a lemon is caused
partly by limonene, an essential
oil in the peel. This group of
organic compounds provides
the smell and color of many
plants. The structure of limonene
has a mirror image (p. 48); this is
found in orange peel. All citrus
fruits contain citric acid (pp. 42-43),
which gives them their tart flavor;
lemons have a greater concentration of
citric acid than is found in oranges.

*Flavor of an orange
comes from hundreds
of compounds*

Chemistry in ancient worlds

EARLY PEOPLE FIRST PRACTICED CHEMISTRY after they learned to use fire. Once fire could be controlled, people began cooking their food and baking clay to produce pottery vessels. Natural curiosity about materials led to experimentation, and ores were smelted to obtain metals. As communities were established, people discovered that particular substances could be used for special purposes. Yeasts were used to prepare beer and wine, and foods were preserved by salting or smoking. Extracts from plants were used to dye clothes, barks provided materials to tan leather, and cosmetics were made from pigments and dyes. Glass, first used as a glaze for beads or pottery, was being blown into shapes by 100 BC. The ancient Egyptians mummified their dead using chemical preparations. The Chinese have a long history of chemical crafts. Lacquer, perhaps the most ancient industrial plastic, was in use in China in an organized industry by 1300 BC. Paper manufacturing and gunpowder were Chinese developments.

FACE PAINTING
People have always used color to decorate themselves and their possessions. This Native American Indian used his warlike face colorings to frighten the enemy and show his status.

Indigo dye, extracted from the leaves of *Indigofera* plant

Saffron from the crocus flower

Red lead decoration

Turmeric

DYES AND DYESTUFFS
Organic dyes such as madder, woad, and indigo attach themselves chemically to textiles. Sometimes the material is treated with a chemical to "fix" the color – this is known as a mordant. Alum (pp. 12-13) was an early mordant. Another method of coloring is to use pigments. Many of these are obtained from minerals that are ground into fine powders for use in cosmetics, paints, and inks.

GREEK PERFUME
Clay is a substance that can be easily molded. When dried and baked, water is lost and chemical changes occur, producing pottery. This perfume bottle has been decorated using pigments such as red lead, which is a lead oxide (pp. 24-25). The perfume was made from oils which were extracted from flowers and spices by gentle heating in oils, such as olive oil.

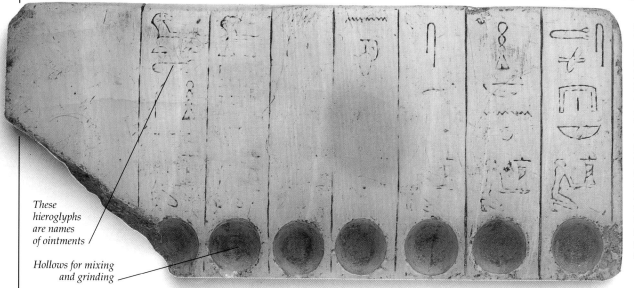

These hieroglyphs are names of ointments

Hollows for mixing and grinding

OINTMENT SLAB
This Egyptian alabaster ointment slab dates from about 2000 BC. Each of the seven hollows is labeled with the name of a cosmetic ointment. The dyes and pigments were ground into fine powders and then mixed with oil, honey, or gum to obtain the right consistency. The Egyptians were also renowned for their use of drugs. For example, they used senna and castor oil as laxatives.

MUMMIFIED CAT

A belief in life after death led the ancient Egyptians to preserve the bodies of their dead. Animals which represented gods were often mummified. This mummy dates from about 1000 BC. First the body was covered with dry natron, a naturally occurring chemical that is chiefly washing soda. This absorbed water from the body, preserving it. After 40 days the body was cleaned, anointed with aromatic resins, and wrapped in linen strips.

Features are painted in kohl, a black pigment derived from antimony (p. 12)

Linen strips woven from flax

Dyed strips

Surface beaten during working

Cutting edge

Barb

Shaft

MAKING GLASS

Glass was probably first made in Egypt around 3000 BC by fusing together sand, soda to lower the melting point, and lime as a stabilizer. The addition of certain metal oxides to the mixture gave colored glass. For example, blue glass could be obtained by adding copper oxide. By Roman times many household vessels were made of glass. This glass bottle was found in a Roman grave. The pearly patina is due to the glass crystallizing with age. The materials for making glass today are little changed since ancient times (pp. 44-45).

Patina

LEATHERMAKING

Hides of animals were valuable materials to early people, but when dried out, raw skin becomes hard. Tanning is a process which combines the skin with substances that preserve it as leather so that it remains flexible when dried. After cleaning and soaking, the leather is treated with extracts of bark, wood, and leaves containing a mixture of special acids called tannins. These react with the protein that makes up skin. After drying, the skins were used for all kinds of purposes – water carriers, harnesses, and shoes, for example.

SUDANESE IRON SPEAR

This barbed spear from the Sudan in Africa dates from the 1930s but was produced by the same methods as spears made 2,000 years before. Iron was harder to extract from its ores than copper or tin because its melting point was too high for early furnaces. The material had to be heated red-hot and worked over and over again to get rid of impurities. Carbon, in the form of charcoal, was added to the ore to improve the properties of the metal, making it easier to sharpen, with a good cutting edge.

Roman glass bottle

EGYPTIAN METALWORKERS

The metalworkers in this Egyptian relief are using blowpipes to make the fire hot enough to melt metal. Gold and silver were used extensively for jewelry. However, bronze – an alloy of copper and tin – was preferred for other articles because it was easier to make and work.

The first chemists

IN ANCIENT GREECE, philosophers began to put forward theories about matter. These theories, mixed with religious ideas and knowledge gained from the chemical crafts of ancient peoples (pp. 10-11), gave rise to alchemy. The alchemists combined mystical ideas of achieving perfection with practical experiments. A belief that one substance could be changed to another led them to seek to change so-called base metals, such as lead, into gold, which was believed to be the most perfect metal. Distillation (pp. 6-7), a technique introduced by these early alchemists, was used to prepare essential oils and perfumes. Later alchemists learned to prepare mineral acids that were much stronger than the acids previously known to them, such as fruit juices. Out of this work, new medical theories developed. The idea arose that disease represented an imbalance of the body's chemical system and should be treated with chemicals to restore the balance. Mining became an important activity; new metals were identified and methods of recognizing them became vital. Techniques of assaying metals – judging their worth – were also developed.

STAR OF ANTIMONY
When antimony is cooled from the molten state, it forms a starry pattern. Its minerals were considered suitable raw material by the alchemists for transmutation of metals (turning them to gold).

GEORGII AGRICOLAE
DE RE METALLICA LIBRI XII

THE IMPORTANCE OF METALLURGY
As mining became economically important, works such as *De Re Metallica* appeared. Written by Georg Bauer (1494-1555), a German physician who used the pen name Agricola, it covered the techniques of mining, smelting to convert the ore to the metal, and assaying, or testing to see what metals were present.

TESTING THE METAL
Assayers worked in the first industrial laboratories in the mining areas of Central Europe, testing minerals for their metal content. They became familiar with a number of chemical reactions, even if they did not understand the chemistry behind them. They had access to a number of chemicals, such as saltpeter (potassium nitrate), alum (potassium aluminium sulfate), and green vitriol (ferrous sulfate). Distilling these together produced *aqua fortis*, or nitric acid, which could be used to separate silver (which dissolved in it) from gold (which did not). *Aqua regia* (concentrated nitric and hydrochloric acids) was used to dissolve gold, leaving silver.

THE ASSAYER'S LABORATORY
A common way of testing the purity of precious metals was by cupellation. The new, smaller furnaces meant that it was possible to maintain a uniform heat for long periods of time. The metal samples, with some lead to help them melt, were placed in a porous cupel, or crucible, and heated in the furnace. Lead and all metals except gold and silver would be converted to the metal oxides (pp. 40-41). These were absorbed by the cupel, which was made of bone ash, leaving a button of the pure gold or silver for testing with acid and weighing.

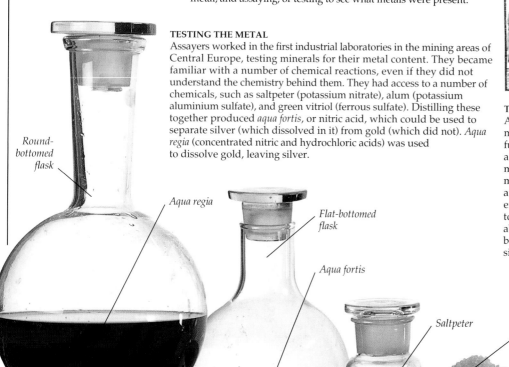

Round-bottomed flask

Aqua regia

Flat-bottomed flask

Aqua fortis

Saltpeter

Alum

Gold button

DISTILLATION APPARATUS

Distillation, or heating liquids to separate them, was an important part of alchemy and many pieces of apparatus were associated with it. The first "still" is thought to have been developed from observations that a pot lid collected condensation. Subsequent apparatus included the retort, which evolved from the alembic (see below). They could be made of glass, metal, or earthenware. The glass was green or brown because of iron impurities in the sand (pp. 44-45).

Glass retort

Early distillation apparatus

Green color from iron impurities in early glassmaking

Substance for distillation placed in here

Long spout helps vapors to condense

Iranian alembic

Alembic head

Condensed vapors collects in rim

Cucurbit

Condensed vapor trickles down the long neck

ESSENTIAL OILS FOR MEDICINE

In the Middle Ages essential oils, such as oil of roses, were obtained by heating extracts of plants in a retort. The oils were vaporized and cooled during their passage down the long neck of the retort to condense in a flask which was often cooled by immersing it in water (pp. 6-7). The furnaces were usually fueled by charcoal.

خشخاش قمب ٣٠. Papaver 142.

حرف الذاٮٯمط XXV. Litera
Adſdſal 149.

AVICENNA'S LEGACY

The word alchemy comes from the Arabic *al kimia*, meaning Egyptian art. The tradition of alchemy spread from Alexandria in Egypt and its language was Arabic. This glossary, with a Latin translation, was compiled by Avicenna (980-1037), a Persian philosopher. It features words such as *alkali* and *alembic*, still part of the language of chemistry today.

THE ALEMBIC

The alembic is an apparatus used in distillation. It comprises the head and the cucurbit (gourd-shaped base) and is believed to have been invented by Maria the Jewess, after whom the bain-marie (water bath), an early source of gentle heat, is named.

STUDYING CHEMISTRY

In the Middle Ages people began to teach the ideas of the alchemists. A new science known as iatrochemistry developed, based on the alchemists' belief that the human body was a chemical system that could be cured with chemicals. Andreas Libavius (1560-1616) published one of the first chemical textbooks, *Alchymia*, in 1597. He documented contemporary findings on pharmacy and metallurgy.

Door for stoking charcoal fire

Furnace

Engraving from *Alchymia*

Cupel made from bone ash

Long-handled metal tongs

CHEMICAL TOOLS

A bone ash cupel, or crucible, and long metal tongs were used to remove metals from a furnace and to pour them into molds. Other tools used by alchemists and assayers are still seen today in laboratories – mortars and pestles (pp. 24-25), flasks, beakers, funnels, and filters.

Alchemical symbols for metals

SYMBOLS FOR SECRECY

Alchemy was closely linked with astrology, and the seven metals known to alchemists shared the symbols of the seven known heavenly bodies. The use of symbols for chemicals arose because of the alchemists' desire to keep their discoveries secret.

Investigating mixtures

EVERYTHING AROUND US IS MADE UP OF CHEMICALS, including ourselves. Some things are made up of a single chemical, or substance. For example, pure water is a substance made up of only one kind of molecule (pp. 16-17). Orange juice, however, contains different kinds of molecules and is a mixture of substances. Vinegar is a solution with water acting as a solvent in which the other substances are dissolved. These substances can be separated physically from one another. Most foods are mixtures. Salad dressing is a mixture, called an emulsion, containing oil and vinegar. They do not mix properly, but separate out into the lighter oily layer and the heavier water layer containing the vinegar. Other kinds of mixtures may be solids, like coins, or gases, like the air around us (pp. 28-29). Toothpaste is a mixture called a suspension, in which fine particles are suspended in a liquid, and they do not dissolve. It is often necessary for chemists to separate out the different chemicals to find out what they are.

SEPARATING LIQUIDS
This separatory, possibly from the 17th century, was used to separate two immiscible liquids (liquids that do not mix) from each other. The heavier liquid is poured off from the bottom, leaving the lighter one behind.

Filter paper

Solid sulfur particles do not pass through filter paper

Filter funnel

Conical flask

MAKING AND SEPARATING MIXTURES
It is possible to extract chemicals from mixtures in several different ways. Filtering and evaporation are two methods demonstrated here. Copper sulfate is a blue salt that dissolves in water – it is soluble. Sulfur is a solid element that does not dissolve in water – it is insoluble.

Beaker

Suspension of sulfur

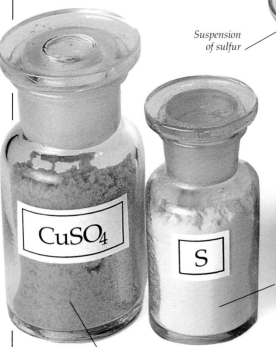

Blue solution of copper sulfate in water

Solution of copper sulfate

Sulfur

Copper sulfate

1 MIXING SUBSTANCES TOGETHER
When copper sulfate and sulfur are added to water, the copper sulfate dissolves, but the sulfur does not. Water is not a solvent for sulfur.

2 SEPARATING THE SULFUR
If the mixture is filtered, the yellow sulfur is easily separated and remains in the filter paper. The water and copper sulfate are not separated. They remain together in a solution. The yellow sulfur can be washed with water to remove any traces of copper sulfate. This technique of filtration is used to extract pure chemicals.

3 HEATING THE SOLUTION
The water can be removed by evaporation to leave blue copper sulfate crystals.

Water lost to atmosphere

Crystals of copper sulfate recovered from solution

Evaporating dish

Wire gauze spreads heat evenly

Bunsen burner

Tripod

Fractionating tower

Low boiling point vapor

Tray holds liquid from condensed vapor

High boiling point vapor

Gases

Condensed gasoline

Diesel fuel

Lubricating oil

Kerosene

Bitumen

Crude oil

CHROMATOGRAPHY
Black ink is a mixture of several different dyes. These can be separated by a technique called chromatography. As the ink and solvent (here water was used) travels up a piece of inked blotting paper, any substances dissolved in it will move up at a rate depending on the size, shape, and chemical characteristics of their molecules.

Different dyes move at different speeds

Blotting paper

Black ink

FRACTIONAL DISTILLATION
Crude oil is the basis of the modern petrochemical industry (pp. 62-63). It contains many different chemical compounds which can be separated into groups using fractional distillation. The crude oil is heated and pumped into the fractionating tower. The vapors cool as they rise. The products from the oil condense when they reach the temperature just below their boiling points and collect on trays. They are drawn off through pipes.

Red wine

THE COMPLETE FOOD
Although milk looks like a uniform liquid, viewed through a microscope it is a mixture of watery liquid with oily drops suspended in it. This mixture is known as a colloid, in which very small particles are dispersed through the liquid but they do not dissolve. The particles are smaller than those in toothpaste, which is a suspension.

ORGANIC MIXTURES
Wine is a complex mixture of organic chemicals (chemicals that are derived from living things), but the differences in it are not clearly seen, even under a microscope: it is homogeneous. Wood is an example of a heterogeneous mixture. It is clear from looking at it that it is not uniform.

Bronze coin

Nickel alloy coin

CURRENCY MIXTURES
Gold, silver, and copper have been used as coinage metals since antiquity, sometimes in mixtures called alloys. Copper, tin, and zinc alloys are used to make bronze coins.

Atoms and molecules

THE IDEA THAT MATTER IS MADE OF tiny indivisible particles was first suggested by the Greek philosopher Democritus (c. 460-370 BC). He called these particles atoms. In the late 18th century a modern theory about atoms originated. By then new gases, metals, and other substances had been discovered. Many chemical reactions were studied and the weights of substances involved were measured carefully. John Dalton's atomic theory arose from these observations. He believed that the atoms of an element (pp. 18-19) were all identical and differed from those of a different element. Two or more of these atoms could join together in chemical combination producing "molecules" of substances called compounds. The molecules in a compound were all identical. The Italian thinker Amadeo Avogadro (1776-1856) asserted that the same volume of any gas would contain the same number of molecules. Although this idea was not immediately accepted, it eventually helped chemists calculate atomic and molecular weights. These weights are related to the weight of hydrogen, which is counted as one (pp. 22-23).

THE NATURE OF MATTER
Englishman John Dalton (1766-1844) was the self-taught son of a Quaker weaver. He was the main advocate of the existence of atoms and his ideas dramatically influenced the study of chemistry. He was interested in everything around him, especially the weather, and began to investigate the marshes near his home in the north of England. He used his experimental findings on gases and those of Antoine Lavoisier (1743-1794) in France. Dalton also devised his own set of symbols for the elements.

Dalton's wooden balls

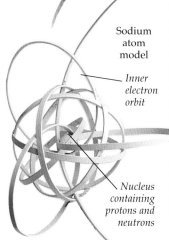

THE FIRST ATOMIC MODELS
Dalton used these balls, the first models of atoms, to demonstrate his ideas. He stated that matter is made up of small indivisible particles, or solid atoms. With the discovery that atoms were surrounded by negatively charged particles called electrons, Dalton's concept of solid atoms began to be less satisfactory.

ATOMS MOVING
Atoms are so small they cannot be seen by the naked eye, but their existence can explain many everyday observations. Look at the way the purple color of the potassium permanganate spreads when its crystals dissolve in water. This is because atoms are constantly moving, so as they come away from the crystals, they move through the water until they are evenly distributed.

ONE VIEW OF AN ATOM
The early years of the 20th century saw the development of ideas about the structure of the atom, with its central nucleus and orbiting electrons. Alongside these developments came an understanding of how atoms bond together to form molecules. Niels Bohr (1885-1962), a Danish physicist, constructed models with fixed orbits; the central nucleus, consisting of protons (positive particles) and neutrons (uncharged particles), had electrons orbiting around it in groups or "shells." This proved to be a convenient and useful model of an atom, but it is not the only view – electrons also behave as if they are waves of energy (like light) and are sometimes best imagined as being spread around the nucleus in a sort of cloud. This Bohr model represents a sodium atom with its nucleus at the center. There are ten electrons in the two inner shells – known as the inner electron orbits – and in the outer electron orbit there is one electron in an incomplete shell. The number of protons in an atom is equal to the atomic number (pp. 22-23).

Sodium atom model

Inner electron orbit

Nucleus containing protons and neutrons

Outer electron orbit

Potassium permanganate crystals added to water

Molecules and measures

Atoms and molecules are tiny, and the number in even a small amount of a substance is huge. To help calculate how many there are, Avogadro's number (6.02×10^{23}) is used as a constant. The amount of a substance containing this number of molecules is called a "mole." Using this measure, the chemical formula (pp. 6-7) can be worked out. Each chemical sample shown here has the same number (Avogadro's) of molecules in it. The weight of each is determined by calculating, in grams, the molecular weight – the atomic weights of all the atoms in the molecule added together.

NaCl

SODIUM CHLORIDE
The atomic weights are sodium 23, chloride 35.5, making the mole weight 58.5 g.

Zn

ZINC
The atomic weight of zinc is 65, making the mole weight 65 g.

$CuSO_45H_2O$

Mercury-filled graduated tube

Thermometer

VAPOR DENSITY APPARATUS
Joseph Gay Lussac (1778-1850) developed this apparatus to measure the weight of the vapor of a compound. The compound was sealed in a glass tube which was heated until it burst and the sample had vaporized. The vapor density was then calculated from the volume of mercury displaced from the tube. From this, the molecular weight and chemical formula can be worked out.

Iron trough filled with mercury

HYDRATED COPPER SULFATE
The atomic weights are copper 63.5, sulfur 32, oxygen 16 (x 4), water 18 (x 5), making the mole weight 249.5 g.

ACETIC ACID
The atomic weights are carbon 12 (x 2), oxygen 16 (x 2), hydrogen 1 (x 4), making the mole weight 60 g. (Indicator has been added to show it is acidic.)

WATER
The atomic weights are hydrogen 1 (x 2), oxygen 16, making the mole weight 18 g.

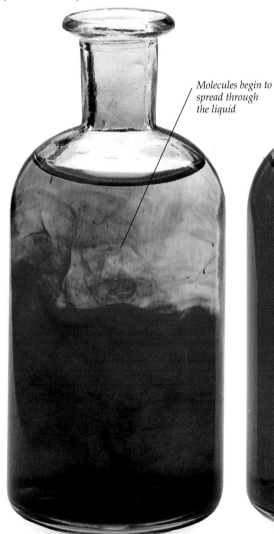

Molecules begin to spread through the liquid

Crystals have dissolved, forming a uniform solution

H_2O

CH_3COOH

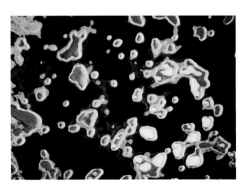

LOOKING AT ACTUAL ATOMS
These uranium atoms cannot be seen with an ordinary microscope – they are too small. An electron microscope uses electron beams instead of light because electrons have shorter wavelengths, allowing smaller objects to be seen. The microscope used here is known as a scanning tunneling microscope.

The elements

AN ELEMENT IS A SUBSTANCE that contains only one kind of atom. Gold contains only gold atoms and hydrogen contains only hydrogen atoms. Water, on the other hand, contains both hydrogen and oxygen atoms and is therefore a compound (pp. 20-21). Antoine Lavoisier (1743-1794) treated elements as substances that could not be broken down into other substances. He produced a list of elements in 1789. Almost all these are found in modern lists, although he also included heat and light. The number of known elements increased during the 18th century as mineralogists analyzed ores and found new metals. New instruments, such as the spectroscope, helped chemists recognize more elements in the 19th century.

THE SCEPTICAL CHYMIST (1661)
The Greeks believed that earth, air, fire, and water were the fundamental elements that made up everything else. Writing in 1661, Robert Boyle (1627-1691) argued against this idea, paving the way for modern ideas of the elements. He defined an element accurately as a substance that could not be broken down into simpler substances.

Green vegetables are a source of sodium, calcium, and iron

Watercress

Apricots

BAUXITE MINE
The claylike mineral bauxite is aluminum oxide (pp. 40-41) from which the element aluminum can be extracted. Here it is being mined in Jamaica. Bauxite is the chief source of aluminum metal (pp. 46-47). Aluminum is used in aircraft parts and engines because it is lightweight, tough, and does not corrode.

Dried fruits are rich in magnesium, calcium, and iron

Berry fruit is a source of folic acid, which helps the absorption of iron

Strawberry

Egg yolk

Nuts and seeds

Seaweed

Sardine

ELEMENTS FROM SPACE
Hydrogen is the simplest element. Over 90 percent of the Universe is made up of hydrogen created at the time of the Big Bang – the explosion that produced the Universe. All other heavier elements have been formed from hydrogen by nuclear reactions. This rock is from a meteorite that collided with the Earth about 20,000 years ago. The elements in it, such as iron and nickel, are identical to those found on Earth or on the Moon, though in different amounts.

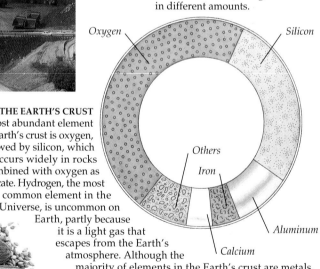

Oxygen

Silicon

Others

Iron

Calcium

Aluminum

THE EARTH'S CRUST
The most abundant element in the Earth's crust is oxygen, followed by silicon, which occurs widely in rocks combined with oxygen as silicate. Hydrogen, the most common element in the Universe, is uncommon on Earth, partly because it is a light gas that escapes from the Earth's atmosphere. Although the majority of elements in the Earth's crust are metals, they account for less than one-quarter of its total mass. Nitrogen forms about four-fifths of our atmosphere (pp. 28-29), but it is so unreactive that it forms only a tiny percentage of the Earth's crust.

TRACE ELEMENTS
Humans need a balanced diet to stay healthy. Tiny amounts of many elements are vital to the chemical processes that go on within us. To prevent deficiencies, staple foods such as bread and margarine often have supplements added to them. Foods from the sea, such as seaweed and oily fish, are rich sources of calcium and iodine. Nuts and seeds are also rich in calcium, which ensures healthy bones and teeth. Egg yolk is a good source of sulfur, sodium, and zinc.

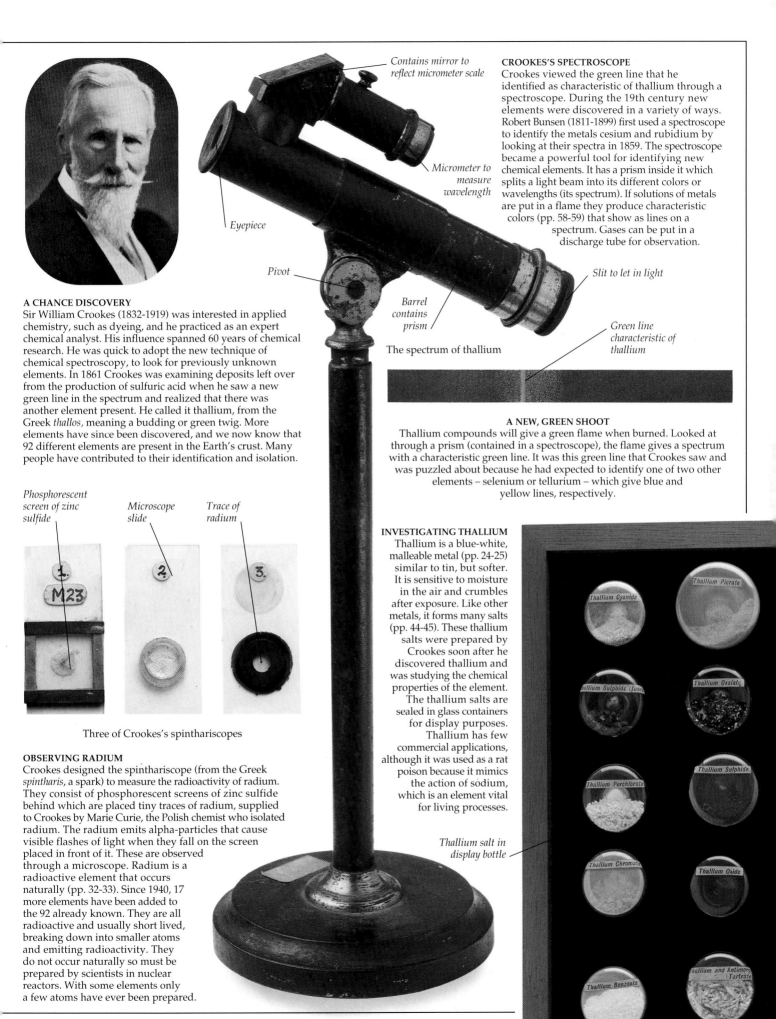

CROOKES'S SPECTROSCOPE

Crookes viewed the green line that he identified as characteristic of thallium through a spectroscope. During the 19th century new elements were discovered in a variety of ways. Robert Bunsen (1811-1899) first used a spectroscope to identify the metals cesium and rubidium by looking at their spectra in 1859. The spectroscope became a powerful tool for identifying new chemical elements. It has a prism inside it which splits a light beam into its different colors or wavelengths (its spectrum). If solutions of metals are put in a flame they produce characteristic colors (pp. 58-59) that show as lines on a spectrum. Gases can be put in a discharge tube for observation.

Contains mirror to reflect micrometer scale

Micrometer to measure wavelength

Eyepiece

Pivot

Barrel contains prism

Slit to let in light

Green line characteristic of thallium

The spectrum of thallium

A CHANCE DISCOVERY

Sir William Crookes (1832-1919) was interested in applied chemistry, such as dyeing, and he practiced as an expert chemical analyst. His influence spanned 60 years of chemical research. He was quick to adopt the new technique of chemical spectroscopy, to look for previously unknown elements. In 1861 Crookes was examining deposits left over from the production of sulfuric acid when he saw a new green line in the spectrum and realized that there was another element present. He called it thallium, from the Greek *thallos,* meaning a budding or green twig. More elements have since been discovered, and we now know that 92 different elements are present in the Earth's crust. Many people have contributed to their identification and isolation.

A NEW, GREEN SHOOT

Thallium compounds will give a green flame when burned. Looked at through a prism (contained in a spectroscope), the flame gives a spectrum with a characteristic green line. It was this green line that Crookes saw and was puzzled about because he had expected to identify one of two other elements – selenium or tellurium – which give blue and yellow lines, respectively.

Phosphorescent screen of zinc sulfide

Microscope slide

Trace of radium

Three of Crookes's spinthariscopes

INVESTIGATING THALLIUM

Thallium is a blue-white, malleable metal (pp. 24-25) similar to tin, but softer. It is sensitive to moisture in the air and crumbles after exposure. Like other metals, it forms many salts (pp. 44-45). These thallium salts were prepared by Crookes soon after he discovered thallium and was studying the chemical properties of the element. The thallium salts are sealed in glass containers for display purposes. Thallium has few commercial applications, although it was used as a rat poison because it mimics the action of sodium, which is an element vital for living processes.

Thallium salt in display bottle

OBSERVING RADIUM

Crookes designed the spinthariscope (from the Greek *spintharis,* a spark) to measure the radioactivity of radium. They consist of phosphorescent screens of zinc sulfide behind which are placed tiny traces of radium, supplied to Crookes by Marie Curie, the Polish chemist who isolated radium. The radium emits alpha-particles that cause visible flashes of light when they fall on the screen placed in front of it. These are observed through a microscope. Radium is a radioactive element that occurs naturally (pp. 32-33). Since 1940, 17 more elements have been added to the 92 already known. They are all radioactive and usually short lived, breaking down into smaller atoms and emitting radioactivity. They do not occur naturally so must be prepared by scientists in nuclear reactors. With some elements only a few atoms have ever been prepared.

Investigating compounds

WHEN ELEMENTS COMBINE, THEY FORM COMPOUNDS. Compounds contain more than one type of atom, bound together to form molecules. A pure compound contains a single kind of molecule. Modern atomic theory helps explain how atoms are held together (bonded) to form molecules. Chemical bonds are formed using the electrons in the outer shell of the atom (pp. 16-17). The atoms either gain, share, or lose their electrons in the process. If one atom gives electrons to another, each then has an electric charge and is attracted to the other like opposite poles of a magnet, forming an *ionic* bond. Metals tend to form ionic bonds. Nonmetals tend to form *covalent* bonds with each other. Instead of handing over electrons to another atom, they prefer to share electrons. Elements that do not give up their electrons, such as the noble gases (pp. 32-33), do not usually react with other elements. They are said to be unreactive, and they do not form compounds easily.

H_2O

Simple formula of water H_2O

Structural formula of water

Ball-and-stick model of water

DOROTHY HODGKIN
The complex vitamin B_{12} molecule contains a total of 181 atoms, compared to water which has three. In 1948 the vitamin was isolated as a red crystalline material; Dorothy Hodgkin (b. 1910) examined it using X-ray crystallography. Together with Alexander Todd (b. 1907), who studied its chemical reactions, they worked out the chemical formula and structure in 1955.

COVALENT BONDS
Covalent compounds may be solids, liquids, or gases at normal temperatures. Water, the commonest and most important compound on Earth, is made up of molecules of two atoms of hydrogen bound to one of oxygen (H_2O). Each hydrogen atom shares its single electron with one from the oxygen, forming covalent bonds.

Space-filling model of water

Positive and negative ions are attracted to one another

Cl

Na

IONIC BONDS
An ion is an atom, or group of atoms with an electric charge. Sodium (Na), a metal, and chlorine (Cl), a nonmetal, react to form an ionic compound – common salt, or sodium chloride (NaCl). The sodium atom gives the single electron in its outer shell to the chlorine atom, completing the chlorine atom's own outer shell. In the crystalline solid of salt, the sodium and chloride ions are arranged alternately in a lattice with ions held together by the electrostatic force of attraction.

MAKING A COMPOUND
In this experiment, iron filings (Fe) are mixed with powdered sulfur (S). Although they are thoroughly mixed, no chemical reaction takes place between them. When heat is applied (step 2), sulfur combines with the iron to form a metal salt – iron, or ferrous sulfide. Metals often form salts with nonmetals (pp. 44-45).

Magnet attracts iron filings

1 MIXING ELEMENTS
The sulfur and iron filings are easily separated using an ordinary magnet that attracts the iron filings, but not the sulfur.

Yellow sulfur powder stays behind

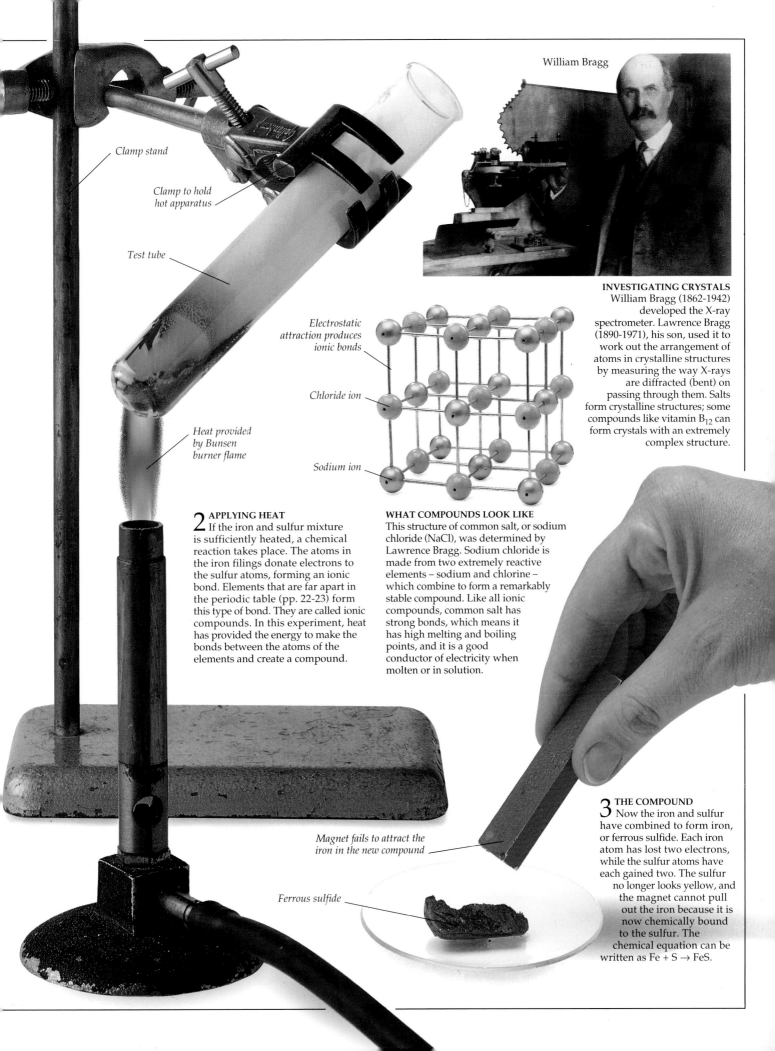

Clamp stand

Clamp to hold
hot apparatus

Test tube

Heat provided
by Bunsen
burner flame

William Bragg

*Electrostatic
attraction produces
ionic bonds*

Chloride ion

Sodium ion

INVESTIGATING CRYSTALS

William Bragg (1862-1942) developed the X-ray spectrometer. Lawrence Bragg (1890-1971), his son, used it to work out the arrangement of atoms in crystalline structures by measuring the way X-rays are diffracted (bent) on passing through them. Salts form crystalline structures; some compounds like vitamin B_{12} can form crystals with an extremely complex structure.

2 APPLYING HEAT

If the iron and sulfur mixture is sufficiently heated, a chemical reaction takes place. The atoms in the iron filings donate electrons to the sulfur atoms, forming an ionic bond. Elements that are far apart in the periodic table (pp. 22-23) form this type of bond. They are called ionic compounds. In this experiment, heat has provided the energy to make the bonds between the atoms of the elements and create a compound.

WHAT COMPOUNDS LOOK LIKE

This structure of common salt, or sodium chloride (NaCl), was determined by Lawrence Bragg. Sodium chloride is made from two extremely reactive elements – sodium and chlorine – which combine to form a remarkably stable compound. Like all ionic compounds, common salt has strong bonds, which means it has high melting and boiling points, and it is a good conductor of electricity when molten or in solution.

*Magnet fails to attract the
iron in the new compound*

Ferrous sulfide

3 THE COMPOUND

Now the iron and sulfur have combined to form iron, or ferrous sulfide. Each iron atom has lost two electrons, while the sulfur atoms have each gained two. The sulfur no longer looks yellow, and the magnet cannot pull out the iron because it is now chemically bound to the sulfur. The chemical equation can be written as Fe + S → FeS.

The periodic table

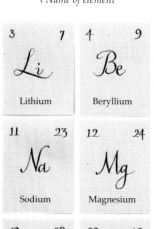

Atomic mass — Atomic number — Chemical symbol — Hydrogen — Name of element

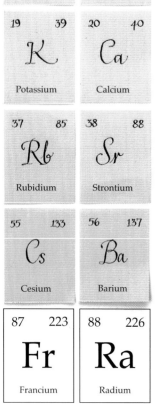

As NEW ELEMENTS WERE DISCOVERED, their atomic masses were determined, and the way each reacted with other substances was studied. Chemists began to notice families of elements that showed similar behavior. As early as 1829 Johann Döbereiner (1780-1849) had introduced the idea of triads of elements (groups of three): thus lithium, sodium, and potassium, all similar metals, formed one group, and they tended to behave in the same way (pp. 24-25). The Russian chemist Dmitri Mendeleyev (1834-1907) observed that elements listed in order of atomic mass showed regularly (or periodically) repeating properties. He announced his Periodic Law in 1869 and published a list of known elements in a tabular form. He had the courage to leave gaps where the Periodic Law did not seem to fit, predicting that new elements would be discovered to fill them.

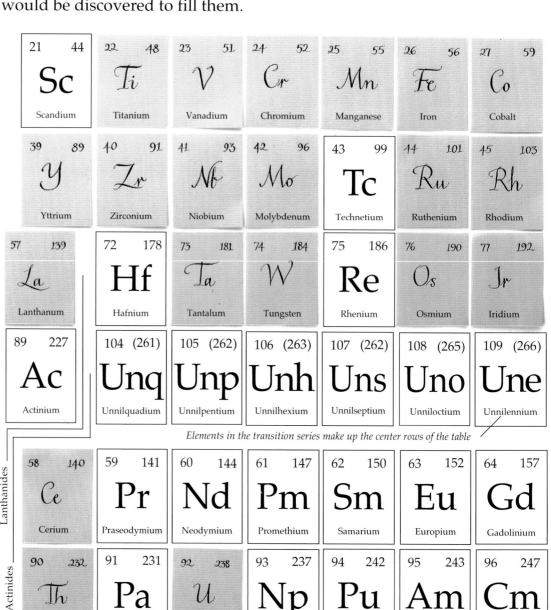

Elements in the transition series make up the center rows of the table

READING THE TABLE
The elements Mendeleyev knew about in his table published in 1871 are shown here as cards. The atoms are arranged in order of increasing "atomic number." This number represents the number of protons (positively charged particles) there are in the nucleus of the atom. This is the same as the number of electrons (negatively charged) surrounding the free atom. Atomic masses are determined by comparing the masses to that of a carbon atom, whose atomic mass is counted as 12.

Lanthanides

Actinides

DMITRI MENDELEYEV
To put some order into his study of the known chemical elements, Mendeleyev made up a set of cards, one for each element, listing their chemical properties. He discovered the Periodic Law while arranging these cards. When he put them in order of increasing atomic masses, the properties were repeated periodically.

Dmitri Mendeleyev

NOBLE GASES (*right*)
No one foresaw the discovery of an entirely new group of elements in the 1890s (pp. 32-33). They were added as a separate column. The periodic table did not immediately have an impact on chemical theory until the discovery of missing elements.

5 11 $\mathcal{B}$ Boron	6 12 $\mathcal{C}$ Carbon	7 14 $\mathcal{N}$ Nitrogen	8 16 $\mathcal{O}$ Oxygen	9 19 $\mathcal{F}$ Fluorine	2 4 He Helium

13 27 $\mathcal{Al}$ Aluminum	14 28 $\mathcal{Si}$ Silicon	15 31 $\mathcal{P}$ Phosphorus	16 32 $\mathcal{S}$ Sulfur	17 35.5 $\mathcal{Cl}$ Chlorine	10 20 Ne Neon

			33 75 $\mathcal{As}$ Arsenic	34 79 $\mathcal{Se}$ Selenium	35 80 $\mathcal{Br}$ Bromine	18 40 Ar Argon

Horizontal rows are known as periods

28 59 $\mathcal{Ni}$ Nickel	29 63.5 $\mathcal{Cu}$ Copper	30 65 $\mathcal{Zn}$ Zinc	31 70 Ga Gallium	32 73 Ge Germanium			36 84 Kr Krypton

46 106 $\mathcal{Pd}$ Palladium	47 108 $\mathcal{Ag}$ Silver	48 112 $\mathcal{Cd}$ Cadmium	49 115 $\mathcal{In}$ Indium	50 119 $\mathcal{Sn}$ Tin	51 122 $\mathcal{Sb}$ Antimony	52 128 $\mathcal{Te}$ Tellurium	53 127 $\mathcal{I}$ Iodine	54 131 Xe Xenon

78 195 $\mathcal{Pt}$ Platinum	79 197 $\mathcal{Au}$ Gold	80 201 $\mathcal{Hg}$ Mercury	81 204 $\mathcal{Tl}$ Thallium	82 207 $\mathcal{Pb}$ Lead	83 209 $\mathcal{Bi}$ Bismuth	84 210 Po Polonium	85 210 At Astatine	86 222 Rn Radon

MODERN NUCLEAR ELEMENTS (*left*)
To avoid disputes over the names of new elements, they have been given systematic names based on their atomic numbers. Therefore, element 104 became unnilquadium from un-nil-quad, or one-zero-four, and so on.

FITTING IN NEW ELEMENTS (*above*)
The crowning achievement of Mendeleyev's periodic table lay in his prophecy of new elements. Gallium, germanium, and scandium were unknown in 1871, but Mendeleyev left spaces for them and even predicted what the atomic masses and other chemical properties would be. The first of these to be discovered, in 1875, was gallium. All the characteristics fitted those he had predicted for the element Mendeleyev called eka-aluminum – because it came below aluminum in his table.

65 159 Tb Terbium	66 162 Dy Dysprosium	67 165 Ho Holmium	68 167 $\mathcal{Er}$ Erbium	69 169 Tm Thulium	70 173 Yb Ytterbium	71 175 Lu Lutetium

97 247 Bk Berkelium	98 251 Cf Californium	99 254 Es Einsteinium	100 253 Fm Fermium	101 256 Md Mendelevium	102 254 No Nobelium	103 257 Lr Lawrencium

INNER TRANSITION SERIES (*left*)
These two rows are known as the lanthanides and actinides after the first members of their groups – lanthanum (atomic number 57) and actinium (atomic number 89). They are traditionally separated out from the rest of the table to give it a coherent shape. The lanthanides are often found together in minerals. They are sometimes called the rare earth elements, although they are not particularly scarce. The actinides are all radioactive. Only the first three are found in nature; the rest have to be made artificially.

Looking at metals

MOST ELEMENTS ARE METALS. Metals are often described as strong, heavy, shiny, and difficult to melt. They are good conductors of heat and electricity and may clang when hit. Many metals are malleable: they can be hammered into shape. Some are ductile: they can be drawn out into thin wires. There are exceptions – mercury is a metal, but is a liquid at room temperature. Metals also have distinctive chemical properties. They react with acids to form salts (pp. 44-45) and with oxygen in the air to form basic oxides (pp. 40-41). Although there are many similarities between metals, there are also differences which determine how appropriate a metal is for a particular use. Some metals are light, such as aluminum, making it ideal as components in the aeronautics industry. Some are resistant to corrosion, such as chromium, which is used for bathroom fittings.

AN ALLOY
The mortar and pestle are essential tools of the chemist and pharmacist. They were often cast by bell founders so they were made from the same metal as bells – an alloy of chiefly tin and copper. An alloy is a mixture of metals (pp. 14-15). Alloys are often preferred to pure metals because they can be mixed to give properties such as rigidity or a low melting point.

LIQUID METAL
This late 18th-century thermometer uses mercury to indicate the temperature. Heat makes the mercury expand. For centuries, it was thought that mercury could exist only as a liquid, but during a cold winter in Russia in 1759 it was observed that mercury froze at about −36.4° F (−38° C).

MINING AND CHEMISTRY
Prospectors looked for mineral deposits and helped identify many new metals. Blowpipes were an important tool in their work. A portable "laboratory" was first described by Karl Friedrich Plattner (1800-1858) in his treatise on blowpipe analysis. This 19th-century set contains mineralogical tools for use in the field. Using the blowpipe for heat, metal samples were fused with lead in a tiny cupel (pp. 12-13) and tested for their reactions with standard chemical reagents.

Bottles containing reagents

Tray holding prospecting tools

Magnifying glass

Wooden case

Bottle containing reagent

Indicator papers

Lead strips

Cupel

Wick

Mortar and pestle

Alcohol burner

Mouthpiece

Blowpipe

SANDSTONE ROCK
This sample of sandstone rock contains a copper ore, which is mainly greenish copper carbonate. Sandstone is a sedimentary rock, which is chiefly silica; the layers of silica in the form of sand have been built up over millions of years. Other substances are mixed in with it as it forms. Analysts find out how much metal is in the rock to determine whether mining will be economically feasible.

ISOLATING THE REACTIVE METALS

Sir Humphry Davy (1778-1829) became a professor at tEngland's Royal Institution in 1801, a year after it was founded. His lectures on scientific topics were very successful, and fashionable society flocked there to listen to him. After the discovery of the voltaic pile (pp. 46-47), Davy built himself a huge battery of voltaic cells and used the electricity they produced to isolate first potassium, then sodium metals from their hydroxides. The following year he isolated magnesium, calcium, strontium, and barium. These metals must be extracted from their molten ores by means of electricity because they are highly reactive. Less reactive metals, for example copper (pp. 44-45), can be extracted from ores by roasting at high temperatures.

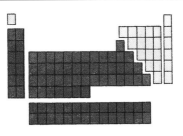

METALS ON THE PERIODIC TABLE

Vertical groups of elements have similar properties. The alkali metals on the left of the table all react with water to form an alkali. The transition metals, which occur from the fourth horizontal row downward, are notable for the variety of colored salts they form.

STRONTIUM

This metallic element is named after the Scottish town Strontian, where ores containing strontium were first found. A soft, silvery metal, it reacts with water and burns in air. Its red flame is used in fireworks. These sample bottles were specially made to fit a display board.

GALLIUM

This metal is soft, silvery, and white, similar to aluminum. Its existence was predicted by Mendeleyev (pp. 22-23). With a low melting point of about 86° F (30° C), it will melt if held in a warm hand. It is extracted by electrolysis as a by-product of bauxite mining (pp. 18-19) and is used in the electronics industry.

How metals react

If an element easily gains or loses the electrons used for bonding (pp. 20-21), it is said to be reactive. All metals can be put in order of their reactivity with water and with air. This is known as the reactivity series, and the order also indicates the ease with which metals can be extracted from their ores. Gold, the least reactive metal, comes at the bottom: it does not react with water, dilute acids, or air, and it is found as the element in nature.

REACTIVITY OF DIFFERENT METALS

Potassium and tin behave differently when put into contact with water. Potassium metal (right) reacts vigorously, and so much heat is generated that the hydrogen gas produced catches fire and burns with a lilac flame. Tin (above), which is lower down the reactivity series, reacts hardly at all with water. If dilute acid is used, potassium reacts even more vigorously, and tin reacts very slowly to produce hydrogen.

Looking at air

GASES FROM BURNING
J.B. van Helmont recognized that different gases could be produced chemically by burning substances. He realized that these gases were different from the air we breathe.

THE AIR AROUND US is made up of a mixture of gases. Oxygen and nitrogen are the two main ones. Most gases cannot be seen or felt. Indeed, until the 17th century people did not realize that there were different gases – there was just air, which was one of the original Greek elements. Johann van Helmont (1577-1644) tried making "airs" chemically. Because his glass apparatus often broke he used the word "gas" for them, which comes from the Greek word for chaos. Investigation of gases started in earnest in the 18th century. The major obstacle was how to handle gases. The pneumatic trough, a device for collecting gases under water or mercury, was introduced by Joseph Priestley and it is still used in laboratories today. The first gas to be studied in detail was carbon dioxide. Joseph Black made it in several different ways and, recognizing that it was not ordinary air, he called it "fixed air." By the end of the 18th century, many of the common gases had been prepared and studied in a science known as pneumatic chemistry.

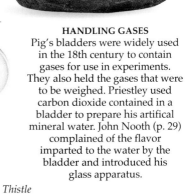

HANDLING GASES
Pig's bladders were widely used in the 18th century to contain gases for use in experiments. They also held the gases that were to be weighed. Priestley used carbon dioxide contained in a bladder to prepare his artifical mineral water. John Nooth (p. 29) complained of the flavor imparted to the water by the bladder and introduced his glass apparatus.

Thistle funnel

Delivery tube

JOSEPH PRIESTLEY (1733-1804)
This medallion of the renowned English clergyman and scientist was made by the English potter Josiah Wedgwood, who also supplied Priestley with much of his chemical apparatus. Using his pneumatic trough, Priestley investigated many gases before his discovery of oxygen. He studied carbon dioxide, obtained as a by-product from the neighboring brewery, and invented a way of preparing carbonated water.

JOSEPH BLACK (1728-1799)
A leading Scottish chemist, Black's careful experiments increased chemical knowledge enormously. His work finally proved that there were other gases besides those present in the atmospheric air. Black first prepared carbon dioxide while studying stomach acidity and how to cure it.

Hydrochloric acid

MAKING CARBON DIOXIDE
In this experiment, carbon dioxide (CO_2) is being prepared by one of the methods used by Joseph Black. Hydrochloric acid is added to magnesium carbonate ("magnesia alba" as Black called it). The resulting gas is collected using a pneumatic trough. Black realized that he could also produce this gas by heating a carbonate, or calcinating limestone. He called it "fixed air" because he recognized that it was not the same as the atmospheric air he breathed, although he did show that small amounts of the gas were present in the atmosphere.

Magnesium carbonate reacting with acid

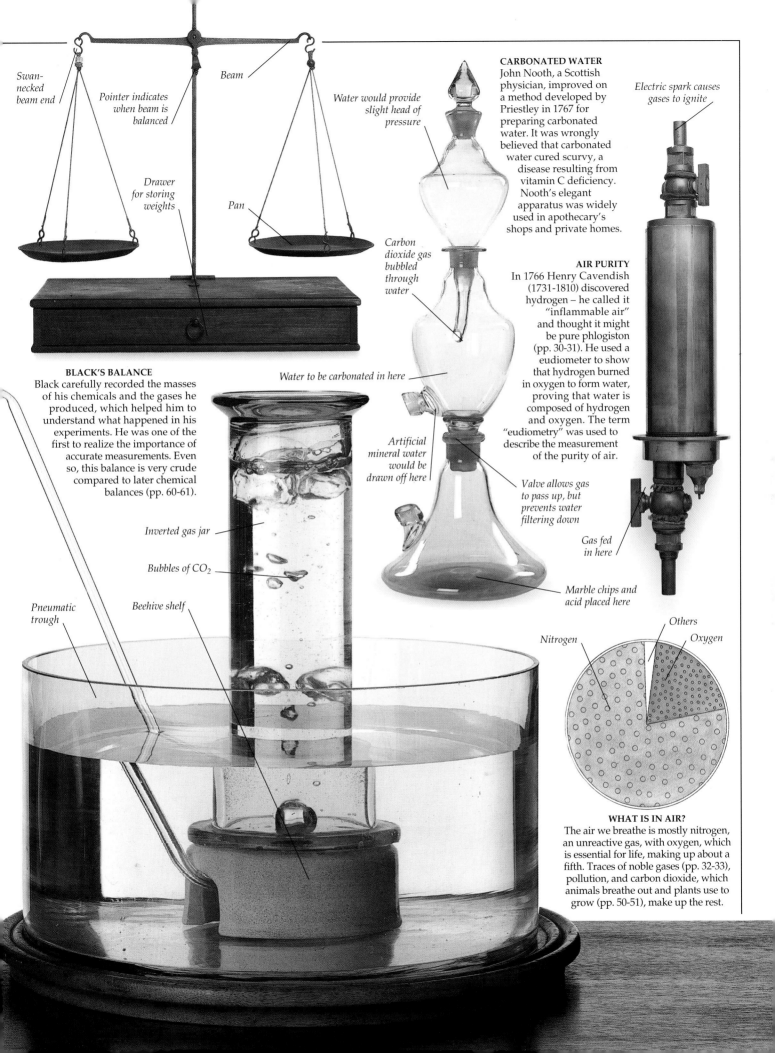

Swan-necked beam end

Pointer indicates when beam is balanced

Beam

Drawer for storing weights

Pan

BLACK'S BALANCE
Black carefully recorded the masses of his chemicals and the gases he produced, which helped him to understand what happened in his experiments. He was one of the first to realize the importance of accurate measurements. Even so, this balance is very crude compared to later chemical balances (pp. 60-61).

Water would provide slight head of pressure

Carbon dioxide gas bubbled through water

Water to be carbonated in here

Artificial mineral water would be drawn off here

CARBONATED WATER
John Nooth, a Scottish physician, improved on a method developed by Priestley in 1767 for preparing carbonated water. It was wrongly believed that carbonated water cured scurvy, a disease resulting from vitamin C deficiency. Nooth's elegant apparatus was widely used in apothecary's shops and private homes.

Electric spark causes gases to ignite

AIR PURITY
In 1766 Henry Cavendish (1731-1810) discovered hydrogen – he called it "inflammable air" and thought it might be pure phlogiston (pp. 30-31). He used a eudiometer to show that hydrogen burned in oxygen to form water, proving that water is composed of hydrogen and oxygen. The term "eudiometry" was used to describe the measurement of the purity of air.

Valve allows gas to pass up, but prevents water filtering down

Gas fed in here

Marble chips and acid placed here

Pneumatic trough

Inverted gas jar

Bubbles of CO_2

Beehive shelf

Nitrogen

Others

Oxygen

WHAT IS IN AIR?
The air we breathe is mostly nitrogen, an unreactive gas, with oxygen, which is essential for life, making up about a fifth. Traces of noble gases (pp. 32-33), pollution, and carbon dioxide, which animals breathe out and plants use to grow (pp. 50-51), make up the rest.

Burning reactions

FIRE PROVIDES HUMANITY WITH LIGHT and heat, the means to cook and to smelt metals. Burning, or combustion, was one of the first chemical reactions to be studied in detail. We now know that when substances burn in air they react with the oxygen in it, forming new compounds and sometimes leaving a residue of ash. Some compounds are gases which disappear into the air; some are solids which remain behind. Early theories assumed that burning wood to form ash was essentially the same as burning metals. In both cases it was believed that burning released part of the original material in the form of phlogiston (from the Greek *phlogistos*, meaning inflammable). This idea proved helpful to the understanding of the chemical processes involved. When products were weighed more carefully, it was realized that although the ash left behind when wood burned was lighter, metals actually increased in weight when burned.

PHLOGISTON THEORY
The German chemist Georg Ernst Stahl (1659-1734) believed that when substances burned they gave up a substance he called phlogiston. This theory proved helpful in explaining reactions, and it diverted many thinkers, but it was proved wrong by Antoine Lavoisier (see below).

Mercury would be heated in retort to form calx

BURNING A CANDLE
Wax is a mixture of compounds containing chiefly carbon and hydrogen. When the wick is lit, some wax is drawn up the wick and vaporizes. The vapor burns, using oxygen in the air. The yellow part of the flame is caused by carbon particles incandescing (glowing) at high temperatures. Unburned carbon forms soot.

Carrying handle

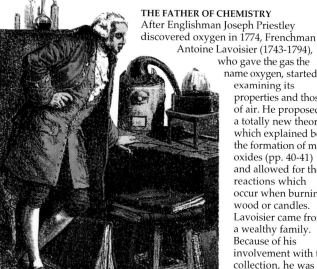

THE FATHER OF CHEMISTRY
After Englishman Joseph Priestley discovered oxygen in 1774, Frenchman Antoine Lavoisier (1743-1794), who gave the gas the name oxygen, started examining its properties and those of air. He proposed a totally new theory which explained both the formation of metal oxides (pp. 40-41) and allowed for the reactions which occur when burning wood or candles. Lavoisier came from a wealthy family. Because of his involvement with tax collection, he was tried and guillotined during the French Revolution.

Opening for fuel

Fire clay furnace

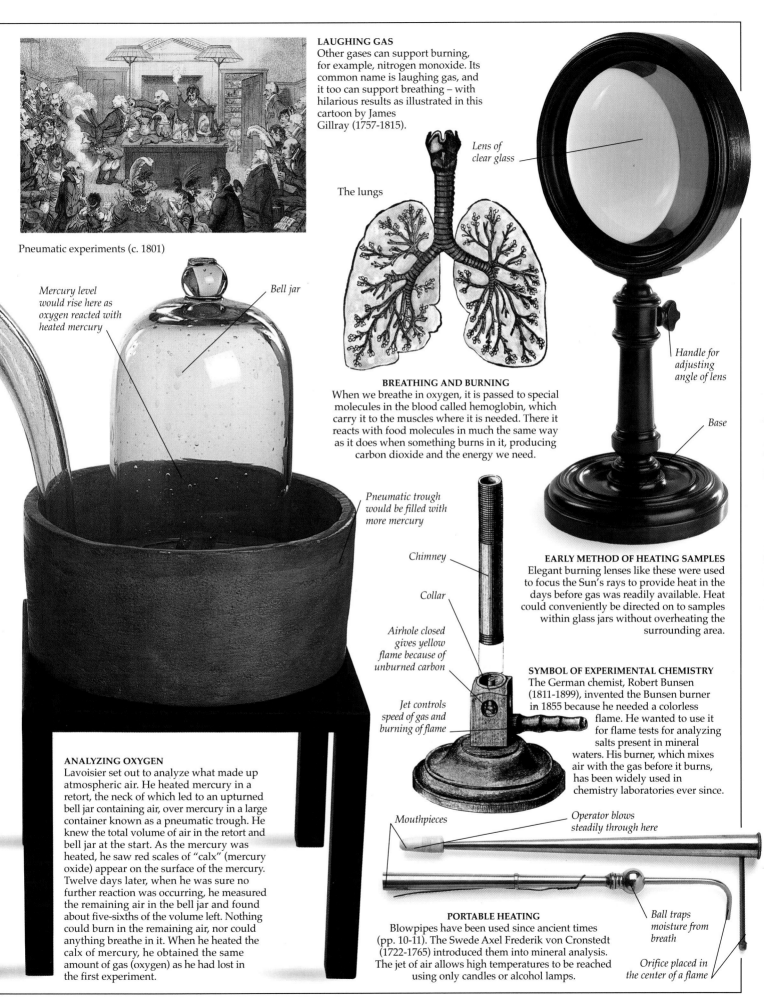

LAUGHING GAS
Other gases can support burning, for example, nitrogen monoxide. Its common name is laughing gas, and it too can support breathing – with hilarious results as illustrated in this cartoon by James Gillray (1757-1815).

Pneumatic experiments (c. 1801)

Lens of clear glass

The lungs

Mercury level would rise here as oxygen reacted with heated mercury

Bell jar

Pneumatic trough would be filled with more mercury

BREATHING AND BURNING
When we breathe in oxygen, it is passed to special molecules in the blood called hemoglobin, which carry it to the muscles where it is needed. There it reacts with food molecules in much the same way as it does when something burns in it, producing carbon dioxide and the energy we need.

Handle for adjusting angle of lens

Base

EARLY METHOD OF HEATING SAMPLES
Elegant burning lenses like these were used to focus the Sun's rays to provide heat in the days before gas was readily available. Heat could conveniently be directed on to samples within glass jars without overheating the surrounding area.

Chimney

Collar

Airhole closed gives yellow flame because of unburned carbon

Jet controls speed of gas and burning of flame

SYMBOL OF EXPERIMENTAL CHEMISTRY
The German chemist, Robert Bunsen (1811-1899), invented the Bunsen burner in 1855 because he needed a colorless flame. He wanted to use it for flame tests for analyzing salts present in mineral waters. His burner, which mixes air with the gas before it burns, has been widely used in chemistry laboratories ever since.

Mouthpieces

Operator blows steadily through here

ANALYZING OXYGEN
Lavoisier set out to analyze what made up atmospheric air. He heated mercury in a retort, the neck of which led to an upturned bell jar containing air, over mercury in a large container known as a pneumatic trough. He knew the total volume of air in the retort and bell jar at the start. As the mercury was heated, he saw red scales of "calx" (mercury oxide) appear on the surface of the mercury. Twelve days later, when he was sure no further reaction was occurring, he measured the remaining air in the bell jar and found about five-sixths of the volume left. Nothing could burn in the remaining air, nor could anything breathe in it. When he heated the calx of mercury, he obtained the same amount of gas (oxygen) as he had lost in the first experiment.

PORTABLE HEATING
Blowpipes have been used since ancient times (pp. 10-11). The Swede Axel Frederik von Cronstedt (1722-1765) introduced them into mineral analysis. The jet of air allows high temperatures to be reached using only candles or alcohol lamps.

Ball traps moisture from breath

Orifice placed in the center of a flame

The noble gases

A~T~ THE START OF THE 1890s, no one had any idea that
there was a separate group of gases in the periodic table
(pp. 22-23), the noble gases. Noble gases are familiar to
us from their use in neon signs and helium balloons.
By 1900 this whole new group had been identified and
isolated. While trying to determine an accurate atomic
mass for nitrogen, British physicist Lord Rayleigh (1842-
1919) discovered that nitrogen prepared from ammonia
was noticeably lighter than nitrogen that came from the
atmosphere. He and William Ramsay (1852-1916) both studied
"atmospheric" nitrogen. By removing the nitrogen from it, they produced a tiny quantity
of another gas. Since it did not react with anything they called it argon, from the Greek
word for lazy. The discovery of helium followed a year later in 1895. Ramsay and his
assistant Morris Travers (1872-1961) then started to search for additional elements in this
new group. They attempted this by fractional distillation
(pp. 14-15) of large quantities of liquid air and argon. In
1898, their efforts were rewarded; they had prepared
krypton, neon, and xenon.

IDENTIFYING HELIUM
During the 1868 eclipse of the Sun
French astronomer Pierre Janssen
(1824-1907) observed a bright yellow
spectral line. This was thought to
signify a new element, named helium
from the Greek word *helios*, the Sun.

THE DISCOVERY OF ARGON
Nitrogen makes up most of the air in our atmosphere. Ramsay
devised this apparatus to absorb all the known gases from atmospheric
nitrogen. Air was first passed over heated copper to remove the oxygen,
and the remaining gases were then passed through the apparatus
which removed moisture, any remaining oxygen, pollutants, carbon
dioxide, and nitrogen, leaving only one-eightieth of the volume of gas
at the end. Ramsay examined this with a spectroscope (pp. 58-59) and
found new spectral lines that did not belong to any known gas. He and
Rayleigh jointly announced the discovery of argon in 1894.

TOEPLER PUMP
This Toepler pump was
used by Ramsay and
Travers to remove air
from their apparatus
and to collect the noble
gases. The violet color
of the glass is due to
irradiation by radon.

SIR WILLIAM RAMSAY
Ramsay was a British
chemist who discovered
argon in collaboration with
the physicist Lord
Rayleigh. In 1904
he received the
Nobel Prize
for chemistry.

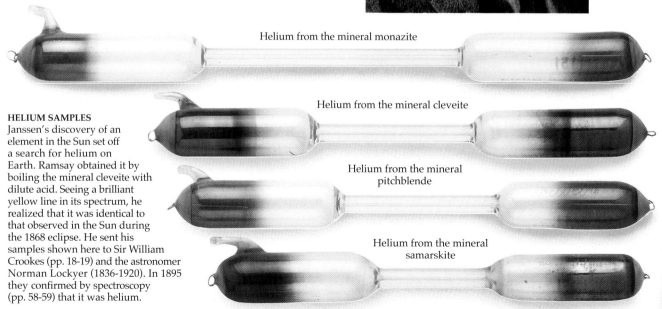

Helium from the mineral monazite

Helium from the mineral cleveite

Helium from the mineral
pitchblende

Helium from the mineral
samarskite

HELIUM SAMPLES
Janssen's discovery of an
element in the Sun set off
a search for helium on
Earth. Ramsay obtained it by
boiling the mineral cleveite with
dilute acid. Seeing a brilliant
yellow line in its spectrum, he
realized that it was identical to
that observed in the Sun during
the 1868 eclipse. He sent his
samples shown here to Sir William
Crookes (pp. 18-19) and the astronomer
Norman Lockyer (1836-1920). In 1895
they confirmed by spectroscopy
(pp. 58-59) that it was helium.

Argon gas

Tungsten filament

Connection to electric current

USING ARGON IN LIGHT BULBS
Since their discovery, the noble gases have found many uses, not least because of their unreactivity. Argon is often used in experiments to provide an inert atmosphere, as here in this light bulb. It does not react with the tungsten filament, even at high temperatures.

THE USES OF HELIUM
As it is much lighter than air, helium is used to fill balloons and airships. Because it does not react (it is inert), it is safer than hydrogen, which can explode in air. The meteorological balloons shown above were used to carry equipment to investigate the hole in the ozone layer above the Arctic in 1990. Some balloons reached an altitude of 18 miles (28 km). Helium is also used to make the voice of the cartoon character Donald Duck. Sound waves travel faster through the light gas and so when the actor breathes helium, his voice becomes high pitched.

Helium-filled balloons

SOURCES OF RADON
Radon, the heaviest noble gas, was first observed as the gas produced by the radioactive element radium when it decayed (pp. 34-35). Some granites used for building houses have been found to give off tiny amounts of radon, which can accumulate in confined areas.

Granite rock

NEON SIGNS
Neon lets off a reddish light when electricity is passed through a vacuum tube containing it. It is used to produce these brightly colored advertising signs in Las Vegas. A high light output is achieved in relation to the power used. Another noble gas, xenon, is used to fill fluorescent tubes and to provide light for lighthouses. Although thought to be unreactive, since 1962 some compounds of xenon have been prepared with highly reactive fluorine (pp. 26-27).

The noble gases

ADDING NEW ELEMENTS
Sir William Crookes devised his own way of representing the periodic table in this elaborate, three-dimensional spiral model made in 1888 before the discovery of the noble gases. However, the model easily fitted in the new group of elements at the center.

BUILDING UP THE PERIODIC TABLE
The noble gases are placed to the right of Mendeleyev's periodic table (pp. 22-23) after the halogen elements. Each gas has a full outer shell of electrons, which explains their lack of reactivity and the reason why they were not discovered sooner.

Chemical reactions

CHEMICAL REACTIONS CAN HAPPEN NATURALLY, without human intervention (pp. 8-9). Reactions happen in living things by making use of proteins called enzymes in complex catalytic reactions (pp. 36-37). Humans can also make chemical reactions happen to provide some of the products we use every day. When a chemical reaction takes place, atoms are rearranged, and new chemical substances are formed. The starting materials in a chemical reaction are called reactants that react to form products. In a chemical reaction there are changes of energy, often in the form of heat. If heat is given off, the reaction is said to be exothermic (potassium in water, p. 25); if heat is absorbed, this is an endothermic reaction (synthesis of fluorine, pp. 26-27). Some chemical reactions are reversible; some are difficult, if not impossible to reverse. In a chemical reaction, a compound may be prepared or synthesized from its elements. For example, iron and sulfur form iron sulfide (pp. 20-21) when they are heated together. A compound can also be broken down – for example, heating metal ores to obtain metals.

THE OZONE LAYER
Ozone is a reactive gas that contributes to pollution when it builds up in the atmosphere over cities. However, ozone in the stratosphere (red here shows maximum ozone concentration) does the useful task of absorbing damaging ultraviolet (UV) light from the Sun, screening it from the Earth. Some synthetic chemicals, especially chlorofluorocarbons (CFCs), react with ozone, creating holes in the ozone layer. These holes allow more UV light through, tending to cause an increase in skin cancer.

USING LIGHT FOR A REACTION
Plants make carbohydrates to build up stems, trunks, leaves, and roots in a process called photosynthesis (pp. 50-51). The plants take in water from the soil, and carbon dioxide from the atmosphere, and use light energy from the Sun to convert them to carbohydrates. They also produce oxygen as a by-product, which they release into the atmosphere through their leaves.

A DISPLACEMENT REACTION
When a coil of copper is dipped into a solution of a silver salt, the copper displaces the silver in the salt. Copper is able to do this because it is higher in the reactivity series of metals (pp. 24-25). Copper and silver nitrate are the reactants in this reaction, and copper nitrate and silver metal are the products. This is called a displacement reaction because one metal has displaced another metal from a solution of one of its salts (pp. 44-45).

1 THE REACTANTS
The coils of copper are dipped into a flask of a silver salt in solution. In this reaction, the salt is the colorless silver nitrate.

Cork stopper

Copper coil

Glass flask

Silver nitrate dissolved in water

2 SILVER COATING
As soon as the copper coil and the salt solution come into contact, the silver is precipitated out of the solution – that is, it becomes an insoluble solid and can be seen as the metal clinging in crystals to the copper strip. The solution turns blue because copper ions displace silver ions in the solution, to produce copper nitrate. The equation can be written as $Cu + 2AgNO_3 \rightarrow Cu(NO_3)_2 + 2Ag$.

Silver crystals grow on the copper coil

Blue copper nitrate is formed in the solution

ROCKET FUEL

The Space Shuttle sits on a large fuel tank holding liquid hydrogen and liquid oxygen in separate containers. They are mixed in the correct proportion and react to provide power. The hydrogen burns in oxygen with a clean flame producing water, seen here as steam.

Glass bottle

Lead nitrate solution

Filter funnel

MAKING A PRECIPITATE

Both potassium iodide and lead nitrate are salts that are soluble in water; they form colorless solutions. However, lead iodide is insoluble, so when the two solutions are mixed, yellow lead iodide is precipitated out of the solution. The other product, potassium nitrate, is colorless and soluble and therefore remains in solution. This is called a precipitation reaction because an insoluble solid is produced during the reaction. This type of reaction is useful for making compounds that are insoluble – the solid precipitate can be filtered off and washed. It can also be used to recognize chemicals in unknown substances (pp. 58-59). The equation can be written as $2KI + Pb(NO_3)_2 \rightarrow 2KNO_3 + PbI_2$.

Lead iodide forms a yellow precipitate

Flask contains potassium iodide in solution

CHEMISTRY IN THE KITCHEN

Like most chemical reactions involving living things, the process of making dough is controlled by enzymes which act as catalysts (pp. 36-37). These start to work as soon as the raising agent, yeast, is mixed with warm water and sugar. (Yeast is a living organism that needs air and moisture to grow; sugar provides food.) Bubbles of carbon dioxide are produced, and when the mixture is added to flour and water to make a dough, the dough rises. Heating kills the yeast and bakes the dough.

Bubbles of gas are trapped in the dough, causing it to expand

The ingredients are left to stand in a warm place

Yeast mixture becomes frothy as carbon dioxide is produced

MODERN ALCHEMY

Ernest Rutherford (1871-1937) was the first person to bombard atoms artificially to produce transmutated elements. The physicist from New Zealand described atoms as having a central nucleus with electrons revolving around it. He showed that radium atoms emitted "rays" and were transformed into radon atoms (p. 19). Nuclear reactions like this can be regarded as transmutations – one element changing into another, the process alchemists sought in vain to achieve by chemical means (pp. 12-13).

Lamp and cigar light up

What drives a reaction?

CHEMICAL REACTIONS SOMETIMES HAPPEN SPONTANEOUSLY; others need energy to make them happen. It is as if reactants have to jump over a barrier to become products. Heat may give them this energy. Light can provide energy, as in photosynthesis (pp. 50-51), and when pollutants react, cause photochemical smogs over our cities. Mechanical energy is sometimes responsible for reactions. Dynamite is usually safe until it is detonated, often by a blast from a detonator which is itself highly sensitive to shock. Reactions can be induced by electrical energy; for the more reactive metals, such as sodium, this is the only practical means of extracting them from their compounds (pp. 46-47). Another way to make a reaction happen is to lower the barrier over which the reactants have to jump. A catalyst does just this by providing a different, easier, path for the reactants to take – it catalyzes the reaction. Often catalysts temporarily combine with a reactant, making it easier for another compound to react with it. In industry, catalysts make processes economically viable by speeding up reactions.

Instantaneous light machine

DÖBEREINER'S LAMP
In 1823 Johann Döbereiner (1780-1849) observed that hydrogen gas caught fire in air if platinum metal was present. He exploited this catalytic reaction in his novelty light machine. When the tap is opened, sulfuric acid drips on to zinc, causing a reaction that produces hydrogen. The hydrogen emerges from the urn, where the platinum catalyst causes it to ignite, lighting a small oil lamp and the cigar.

CLEANING UP THE ENVIRONMENT
Car exhaust fumes are a source of pollution. Exhaust fumes contain poisonous gases, such as carbon monoxide, and gases that contribute to smog. Catalytic converters dramatically reduce the amounts of these gases emerging from car exhausts. They contain precious metals – the catalysts – which catalyze reactions that convert the gases to harmless ones. Catalysts are easily poisoned: lead is one such poison, so catalytic converters can be fitted only to cars using unleaded gasoline.

1 POISONOUS PRODUCTS
When petrol burns, the main products are carbon dioxide and steam. Also formed are nitrogen oxides (some nitrogen in the air reacts at the high temperatures of the engine), carbon monoxide from incompletely burned hydrocarbon, and fragments of unburned hydrocarbons. From the engine, these gases are passed straight into the catalytic converter.

Pollutant gas includes carbon monoxide, nitrogen oxides, and fragments of unburned hydrocarbons

Gases pass straight from engine into the converter

Glass negative
(1890s)

Black-and-white print

CHEMICALS USED FOR PHOTOGRAPHY
These 19th-century glass negatives were covered with a sticky solution of potassium iodide. Immediately before exposure, they are dipped in silver nitrate solution to form light-sensitive silver iodide. When light falls on the plate during exposure, the molecules of silver iodide are activated by the energy from the light. The plate is then developed by immersing it in a solution that converts the activated silver salt to metallic silver particles so fine they look black. Objects that reflect most light on to the plates show as dark areas in the negative, while those that do not reflect light are transparent.

MAKING A PRINT
Light is shone through the glass negative on to paper coated with another chemical – silver chloride. Where the negative is dark, no light reaches the paper and the silver salt is not activated, but where the negative is transparent, light activates the silver salt. When the paper is developed and fixed with more chemicals, the activated areas react to give dark silver where the negative was transparent, and light areas where the negative was dark.

ENZYMES AT WORK
Almost all reactions that take place in living things are directed by enzymes – biological catalysts. Amylase is an enzyme in saliva that starts to break down starch molecules from food into sugar units that provide our energy. It starts to work as soon as the food is in the mouth. Lysozyme is another enzyme, found in tears. It attacks the cell walls of bacteria, preventing them from infecting the eye.

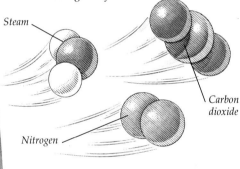

Steam

Carbon dioxide

Nitrogen

3 CLEAN AIR
By the time the gases reach the exhaust, the nitrogen oxides have been converted back to nitrogen by rhodium (one of the platinum metals); platinum has catalyzed the unburned hydrocarbons and the carbon monoxide to steam and carbon dioxide. With an efficiently running engine, the converter can remove up to 95 percent of pollutants.

Steel casing

Thin layer of platinum and rhodium catalysts coat ceramic honeycomb

USING FRICTION IN A REACTION
"Strike anywhere" matches contain the nontoxic red form of phosphorus (pp. 26-27) with sulfur in the head. When the match is struck on a rough surface, the friction provides the energy that causes the phosphorus to ignite.

Friction causes phosphorus to ignite

2 HONEYCOMB STRUCTURE
The stainless steel casing of the catalytic converter houses a ceramic honeycomb structure. So fine is this honeycomb that it provides a surface area as large as about two football pitches on which the catalytic reactions take place. Although the metal catalysts are rare and expensive (platinum metals are used), only $\frac{1}{14}$ oz (2 g) are required to coat the honeycomb with a thin layer. This is enough to clean up exhaust gases for 50-100,000 miles (80-160,000 km).

Rates of reaction

SOME CHEMICAL REACTIONS TAKE PLACE ALMOST INSTANTLY – the reactions of explosives, for example. Others can proceed so slowly it may take years to see the results. Reactions will take place only when the reacting molecules come into contact with each other. Increasing the number of times molecules collide with each other will therefore increase the speed of a reaction. This can be done by increasing the amount of surface area so that more reactant is exposed. In a solution, the same effect is achieved by increasing the concentration – the number of molecules of compound in the solvent. Adding heat can speed up most reactions. This makes the molecules move around more quickly, so they collide more often. Catalysts are another way of speeding up a reaction. All these factors are taken into account in industrial processes, where time and economics play an important part. In theory, all reactions could proceed in either direction, but in practice many reactions are difficult to reverse. Those that proceed in either direction are said to be reversible and the amounts of reactants and products will reach equilibrium.

INSTANT REACTION
The spectacular displays provided by fireworks are initiated by the burning of gunpowder, a very fast reaction. Strongly exothermic (p. 34), this reaction gives out the heat required to cause the metal atoms to emit characteristic colors (pp. 58-59).

REACTION TAKING YEARS
Although copper is fairly resistant to corrosion, it slowly reacts with moisture and carbon dioxide in the air to form the hydrated green carbonate. This green coating can often be seen on copper roofs. In industrial areas, basic copper sulfate is also formed due to sulfur dioxide in the air (p. 6).

INCREASING THE SPEED
When hydrochloric acid is added to chips of marble (a naturally occurring form of calcium carbonate), bubbles of carbon dioxide gas are produced. The acid reacts when it comes into contact at the surface of the marble. If the marble is ground up into a fine powder, its surface area is increased enormously, and the reaction goes so fast that the bubbles cause the reactants to fizz up and overflow.

Glass beaker

Carbon dioxide gas gently bubbles to the surface

Chips of marble

Only the outer surface of the marble chips have reacted with acid

Gas bubbles up rapidly, causing spillage

Ground marble

LE CHATELIER'S PRINCIPLE

Henri Louis Le Chatelier (1850-1936) was a French professor of chemistry. He studied the gases that caused explosions in mines and the reactions that occur in a blast furnace (pp. 40-41). These studies led him to put forward the principle that bears his name. This principle explains that if conditions such as temperature or pressure are changed in a system containing reactants and products, then any chemical reaction occurring will tend to counteract the change and return the conditions to equilibrium.

Henri Le Chatelier

HELPING THE WAR EFFORT

Fritz Haber (1868-1934), a German chemist, succeeded in manufacturing ammonia from nitrogen and hydrogen gases using a catalyst (pp. 36-37) of osmium. Saltpeter was used to prepare nitric acid, needed for the manufacture of explosives. During the World War I Germany's supplies of saltpeter from Chile were cut off. However, ammonia could be oxidized to nitric acid, so the new Haber process ensured the continuing supplies of explosives. Haber used Le Chatelier's principle to work out the best conditions of temperature and pressure. Only 10-20 percent of the nitrogen and hydrogen combine, so the gases are recycled.

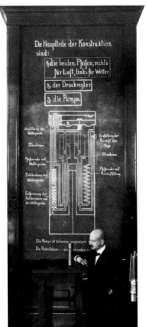

Fritz Haber

REVERSIBLE REACTIONS

A reversible reaction can go in either direction. The products that are formed during the reaction are able to react with each other and re-form the reactant. This experiment demonstrates that the formation of dichromate ions from chromate ions is reversible.

Pipette

Drop of hydrochloric acid

1 A REACTANT
Potassium chromate dissolves in water to form a bright yellow solution containing potassium and chromate ions.

2 THE REACTION
Hydrochloric acid is added to the potassium chromate a drop at a time. The solution begins to turn bright orange, as the acid causes a chemical reaction to take place. The chromate ions in the solution are turned into orange dichromate ions, making another salt, potassium dichromate.

Pipette

Drop of sodium hydroxide

Sodium hydroxide neutralizes the acid

Potassium chromate dissolved in water

Adding acid turns the solution orange

3 REVERSING THE REACTION
Sodium hydroxide, which is a base (pp. 42-43), is added a drop at a time to remove the acid by neutralizing it. The solution is returning to the original bright yellow color as the chromate reforms. The equilibrium was disturbed by changing the amount of a reactant.

Oxidation and reduction

FLASH PHOTOGRAPHY
Magnesium metal was produced commercially from the 1860s as wire or ribbon. It readily burns in air, the metal being oxidized to magnesium oxide. The brightness of the white flame made it useful in photography to provide studio lighting.

WHEN OXYGEN COMBINES WITH A REACTANT (pp. 34-35), an oxidation reaction has taken place. Oxygen in the air frequently causes oxidation, either rapidly, by burning substances, or more slowly, in reactions such as rusting. The removal of oxygen from a reactant is called reduction. Extracting iron from its oxides (compounds containing iron and oxygen) in iron ore is a reduction reaction. If one reactant is oxidized while the other is reduced, it is called a redox (*red*uction-*ox*idation) reaction. The removal of hydrogen from a compound is also a type of oxidation: fluorine is obtained by oxidizing hydrogen fluoride (pp. 26-27). The addition of hydrogen is a reduction reaction. This happens during the hydrogenation of fats to make margarine (p. 7). Oxidation is a cause of food deterioration: the cut surface of an apple quickly browns in air.

Molten pig iron poured in here

Steel shell of converter

Lining made from silica firebricks to withstand heat

BESSEMER PROCESS
Most metals produced by reducing metal ores need further purification. Iron is produced by reducing iron ore (mostly oxides) with coke in a blast furnace. The resulting pig iron contains mainly carbon, silicon, and phosphorus. The conversion of this brittle metal to steel was revolutionized by the introduction of the Bessemer process by 1857. However, the iron ore from some localities contained large amounts of phosphorus that were not all removed in Bessemer's process. In 1878, the metallurgist Sidney Thomas suggested lining the converter with dolomite (a carbonate ore). This reacted with phosphorus to form phosphates, which were absorbed into the lining.

SIR HENRY BESSEMER (1813-1898)
A British engineer, Bessemer revolutionized the process of converting cast iron directly to steel by burning out the impurities in his steel converter. The shorter process and lower production costs made steel readily available in large quantities for the first time.

Converter pivoted to the horizontal to receive molten iron

1 LOADING THE FURNACE
The converter is filled with about 30 tons of molten pig iron together with fluxes such as limestone and fluorite to help extract the impurities in the form of molten slag. Initially, the process was carried out in a fixed converter. This more efficient moving converter, which could tilt to receive the metal, was introduced in 1860.

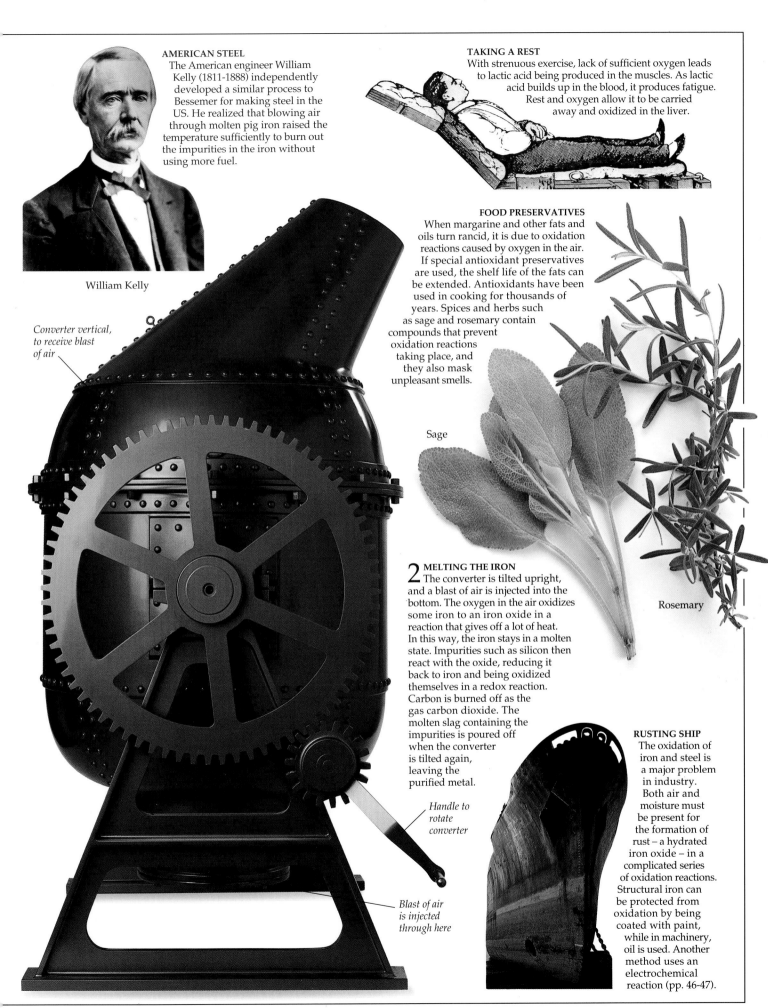

AMERICAN STEEL
The American engineer William Kelly (1811-1888) independently developed a similar process to Bessemer for making steel in the US. He realized that blowing air through molten pig iron raised the temperature sufficiently to burn out the impurities in the iron without using more fuel.

William Kelly

TAKING A REST
With strenuous exercise, lack of sufficient oxygen leads to lactic acid being produced in the muscles. As lactic acid builds up in the blood, it produces fatigue. Rest and oxygen allow it to be carried away and oxidized in the liver.

FOOD PRESERVATIVES
When margarine and other fats and oils turn rancid, it is due to oxidation reactions caused by oxygen in the air. If special antioxidant preservatives are used, the shelf life of the fats can be extended. Antioxidants have been used in cooking for thousands of years. Spices and herbs such as sage and rosemary contain compounds that prevent oxidation reactions taking place, and they also mask unpleasant smells.

Sage

Rosemary

Converter vertical, to receive blast of air

2 MELTING THE IRON
The converter is tilted upright, and a blast of air is injected into the bottom. The oxygen in the air oxidizes some iron to an iron oxide in a reaction that gives off a lot of heat. In this way, the iron stays in a molten state. Impurities such as silicon then react with the oxide, reducing it back to iron and being oxidized themselves in a redox reaction. Carbon is burned off as the gas carbon dioxide. The molten slag containing the impurities is poured off when the converter is tilted again, leaving the purified metal.

Handle to rotate converter

Blast of air is injected through here

RUSTING SHIP
The oxidation of iron and steel is a major problem in industry. Both air and moisture must be present for the formation of rust – a hydrated iron oxide – in a complicated series of oxidation reactions. Structural iron can be protected from oxidation by being coated with paint, while in machinery, oil is used. Another method uses an electrochemical reaction (pp. 46-47).

Acids and bases

IN NATURE, ACIDS CAN BE FOUND IN FRUITS: citric acid is responsible for the sharp taste of lemons (p. 9). Vinegar contains acetic acid, and tannic acid from tree bark is used to tan leather (p. 11). The stronger mineral acids have been prepared since the Middle Ages. One of these, *aqua fortis* (nitric acid), was used by assayers to separate gold from silver (pp. 12-13). Car batteries contain sulfuric acid, also strong and corrosive. A base is the opposite of an acid. Bases often feel slippery; bicarbonate of soda and soap are bases, and so is lye, a substance that can burn skin. Bases that dissolve in water are called alkalis. In water, acids produce hydrogen ions (pp. 20-21), while alkalis produce hydroxide ions.

When an acid and a base react together, the hydrogen and hydroxide ions combine and neutralize each other, forming water together with a salt (pp. 44-45). The strength of acids and bases can be measured on a pH scale.

WATER SPLITTING
Pure water is neither acidic nor basic: it is neutral. It can split (dissociate) into two ions: a positively charged hydrogen ion (H^+) and a negatively charged hydroxide ion (OH^-). In solutions of acids, there are more hydrogen ions than hydroxide ions. In solutions of alkalis, hydroxide ions outnumber the hydrogen ions.

Water molecule
H_2O

Hydrogen ion H^+

Hydroxide ion OH^-

CHOOSING THE COLOR
The compounds responsible for color in plants are often sensitive to acids and alkalis. Blue hydrangeas grow only in acidic soils; in neutral or alkaline soils, they will revert to pink.

Pink hydrangea from alkaline soil

Hydrangea is blue in acidic soil

STRONG ACIDS
Dilute hydrochloric acid, like other mineral acids such as sulfuric and nitric acids, has a pH of about 1.

SHARP TASTES
Vinegar contains acetic acid. This acid is also produced when wine is exposed to the air. It has a pH of about 4.

Hydrochloric acid

Vinegar

Chart for universal indicator papers

Color codes

S.P.L. Sørensen (1868-1939) introduced the pH scale to measure the concentration of hydrogen ions in solution. The more hydrogen ions, the stronger the acid. The amount of hydrogen ions in solution can affect the color of certain dyes found in nature. These dyes can be used as indicators to test for acids and alkalis. An indicator such as litmus (obtained from lichen) is red in acid. If a base is slowly added, the litmus will turn blue when the acid has been neutralized, at about 6-7 on the pH scale. Other indicators will change color at different pHs. A combination of indicators is used to make a universal indicator. Here universal indicator papers have been used with a range of pH from 2-11 (some papers measure 0-14). Starting with pink for strong acids below pH 2, it goes through various colors to green at the neutral pH 7 and to dark purple for strong alkalis at pH 11 and above.

FORENSIC SCIENCE

Chemistry often comes to the aid of the forensic scientist when solving a crime. The pH of soil samples from a suspect's shoes or perhaps from the tread of a car tire can be measured to compare it with soil at the scene of the crime. Samples of the two soils are mixed thoroughly with distilled water (with a neutral pH), then filtered. Drops of universal indicator solution change the color according to acidity. This color is then compared with those on a chart, to find out the precise pH of the soils.

RECOGNIZING ACIDS

Svante Arrhenius (1859-1927), a Swedish scientist, won the 1903 Nobel Prize for his work on ionization. He introduced the idea of compounds dissociating, or splitting, into their constituent ions in solution. He explained how the strength of acids in aqueous (water) solution depended on its concentration of hydrogen ions.

Filter paper traps solid soil particles

Distilled water with soluble material from soil

Svante Arrhenius

Universal indicator solution

Soil sample mixed with distilled water

Universal indicator turns the solution orange – a mildly acidic soil

Dropper

DRINKING WATER
Tap water has a pH of 6. It changes with the area but is usually slightly acid because of dissolved materials. Pure water is neutral at pH 6-7.

CLEANING MATERIALS
Soaps are made by reacting organic acids with a strong base. Because the organic acid is weak, soaps are mildly basic with a pH of 8-9.

HOUSEHOLD CLEANER
Household cleaners range in strength depending on their purpose. Oven cleaners contain lye. This brand contains ammonia and is pH 10.

Tap water

Liquid soap

Household cleaner

Forming salts

SALTS CAN BE PREPARED BY MIXING an acid with a base (pp. 42-43) or a metal. If the acid is sulfuric acid, the salt is called a sulfate; hydrochloric acid forms salts called chlorides; nitric acid forms salts called nitrates. Salts are ionic compounds (pp. 20-21) consisting of a positive ion, usually a metal, and a negative ion, which may be a nonmetal or a group of atoms bound together. The best known salt is probably sodium chloride – an essential part of our diet. Not all salts are harmless; thallium salts (pp. 18-19) were used as rat poison. If allowed to form slowly, salts become regularly shaped crystals. Some are soluble in water; some are not. Their solubility can be used to determine which metals are present in substances (pp. 58-59). Some salts take up water from the air; they are deliquescent. Some salt crystals gradually lose their attached water; they are efflorescent (washing soda). Sometimes salts come out of solution in inconvenient ways: kettles and central heating pipes become clogged up with calcium and magnesium salts in areas with hard water.

COMMON SALT
Sodium chloride is called common or table salt. Traces of another edible salt – magnesium carbonate – are added to help it flow.

PRECIOUS IMPURITIES
Emerald is mainly the colorless mineral beryl. It owes its green color to the presence of tiny amounts of the green salt, chromium oxide. Rubies are chiefly made up of aluminum oxide in the form of corundum (a hard, natural mineral). Pure corundum is colorless, and ruby gets its red color from the same chromium salt because it is forced into the crystal structure of corundum, causing its spectrum to shift slightly.

Ruby

Emerald

SALTS FROM COPPER
The metal copper, like other metals, forms a wide variety of salts. The copper salts shown here can be prepared in many different ways. Copper oxide (CuO) can be prepared by heating the metal with air. It is used as a pigment. Copper carbonate ($CuCO_3$) will yield carbon dioxide and copper oxide on heating. The green color on copper roofs is a form of copper carbonate (p. 38). Copper chloride ($CuCl_2$) is soluble in water. It is used as a catalyst. Copper hydroxide ($Cu(OH)_2$) comes out of solution when alkali is added to soluble copper salts. Copper sulfate ($CuSO_4.5H_2O$) forms hydrated crystals (containing water molecules). It is used in agriculture as a fungicide. Copper nitrate ($Cu(NO_3)_2$) is very soluble and will even take up water from the air and dissolve itself.

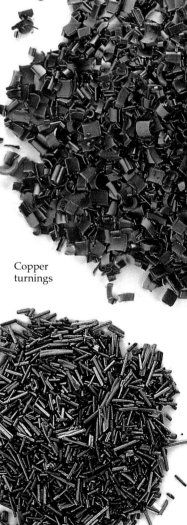

Copper turnings

Copper oxide

Cap traps waterborne solids

Ion-exchange resin removes positive and negative ions

Charcoal absorbs organic pollutants such as pesticides

Final filter for any remaining waterborne solids

Positive metal ions are trapped and replaced with hydrogen ions (H^+)

Negative ions are trapped and replaced with hydroxide ions (OH^-)

The H^+ and OH^- ions combine to form water (H_2O)

Treated water

PURIFYING WATER
Tap water contains a number of impurities that impair the taste, cause the buildup of scale in kettles, and form a scum with soaps. Many impurities are salts that can be removed by a process called ion exchange. This uses a resin made up of small plastic beads with ions bonded to their surface. They replace positive metal ions, such as aluminum and calcium, with hydrogen ions, and they replace negative ions, such as nitrate, with hydroxide ions. Hydrogen and hydroxide ions make up water.

Copper sulfate

Copper
nitrate

*Airtight
seal*

*Rock salt
prism*

Silica gel

KEEPING A PRISM DRY
The prism in this desiccator is made of rock
salt and is used for spectroscopy (p. 59). It
must be kept absolutely dry; otherwise, it will
deteriorate. The atmosphere is kept dry using
silica gel, a hydrated form of silicon dioxide
that absorbs water very efficiently. It is
colored blue by another salt, cobalt chloride,
which turns pink in the presence of water.

Copper
hydroxide

*Sodium
carbonate*

Limestone

Sand

THE INGREDIENTS IN GLASS
Glass is made from several salts. The
main constituent is silicon dioxide in
the form of sand. Limestone (calcium
carbonate) and sodium carbonate are also
added to make the common soda glass
used for bottles. The greenish tinge of old
glass (p. 13) is due to iron impurities in
the sand. Other metal salts can be added
to the mix to make colored glass.

Copper chloride

Copper carbonate

45

Electricity and chemistry

CHEMICALS ARE USED TO PRODUCE ELECTRICITY; and electricity can produce chemicals. Alessandro Volta succeeded by 1800 in making electricity with the first battery, using different metals separated by salt solutions. Investigations of the effects of passing electricity from these batteries through solutions (electrolytes) began immediately. It was found that passing a current through water separated it into hydrogen and oxygen gases, the elements that make up water. Michael Faraday (1791-1867) showed that pure water does not conduct electricity well, but if salts are added, conductivity increases. This is because the electricity is carried by ions in the solution; water is a poor conductor, or electrolyte, because it is only slightly ionized (pp. 20-21). Salts, acids, and bases (pp. 42-45) are good electrolytes. Electricity is also used to produce chemicals in electrolytic cells, and to purify substances.

Zinc disc

Copper disc

Cardboard disc soaked in brine

A voltaic pile

THE FIRST BATTERY
Alessandro Volta (1745-1827), an Italian scientist, noticed that two different metals in contact produced a "bitter taste" when they touched his tongue. Further experiments convinced him this was caused by an electric current. Volta found he could generate electricity by putting a layer of cardboard soaked in brine between discs of copper and zinc – a voltaic cell. When he made a "pile" of these cells, he increased the amount of electricity generated. This was the first battery – a collection of cells.

PIONEER OF ELECTROLYSIS
Humphry Davy (1778-1829) started studying electrochemistry soon after the introduction of the voltaic cell. He succeeded in extracting sodium and potassium metals from their hydroxides, which had previously resisted all attempts to break them down to simpler substances. Davy also isolated other metals, such as strontium (p. 25), by electrolysis.

Steel clip   Copper layer   Nickel layer   Gold finish

COATING METALS
Electroplating is used to give attractive and durable finishes to metals. The gold finish on this pen clip involves several stages. The steel clip is suspended from the cathode (the negative terminal) and then dipped into the electrolyte – copper cyanide. The cyanide cleans the steel, while the copper layer provides a better base for further electrolysis. A layer of nickel plating ensures a bright final product and improves resistance to corrosion. The gold plating is the final layer.

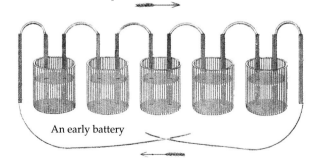

An early battery

A FLOWING CURRENT
This early battery has zinc and copper electrodes dipping into cups of salt solution (the electrolyte). When the electrodes are connected, zinc dissolves, losing electrons, while hydrogen ions at the copper electrode gain electrons to form hydrogen gas. These reactions cause a current to flow.

SPLITTING SALT
The electrolysis of brine (concentrated sodium chloride) is a major industrial process. These huge cells are used to pass current through the brine. The chemical products are chlorine and hydrogen gases, and sodium hydroxide (lye).

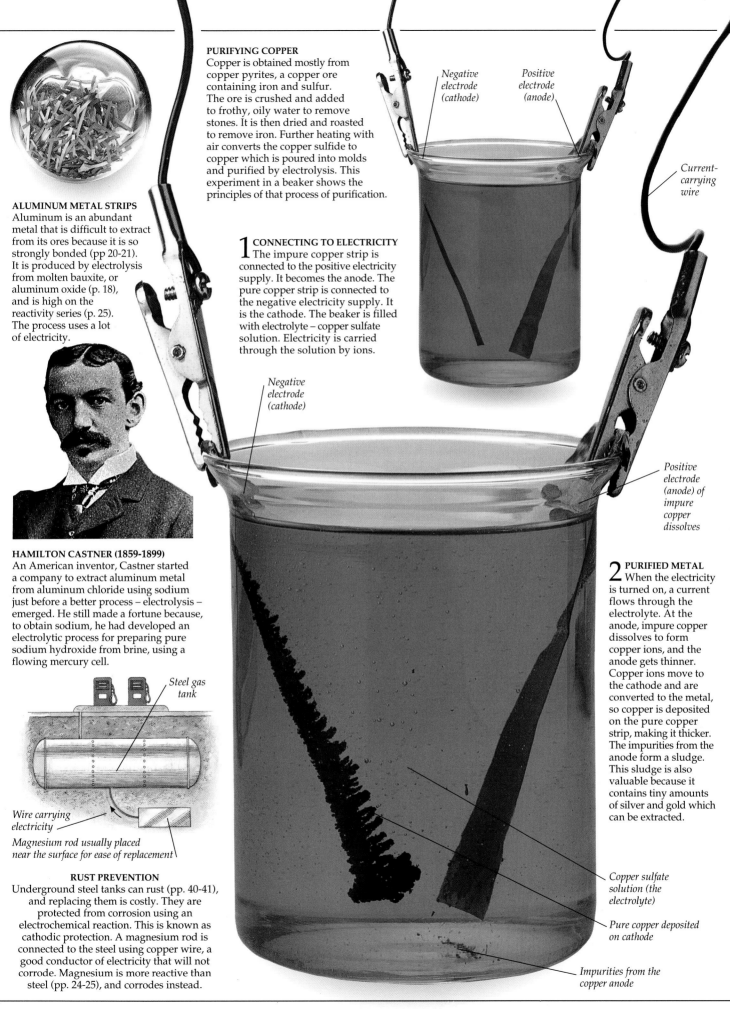

ALUMINUM METAL STRIPS
Aluminum is an abundant metal that is difficult to extract from its ores because it is so strongly bonded (pp 20-21). It is produced by electrolysis from molten bauxite, or aluminum oxide (p. 18), and is high on the reactivity series (p. 25). The process uses a lot of electricity.

HAMILTON CASTNER (1859-1899)
An American inventor, Castner started a company to extract aluminum metal from aluminum chloride using sodium just before a better process – electrolysis – emerged. He still made a fortune because, to obtain sodium, he had developed an electrolytic process for preparing pure sodium hydroxide from brine, using a flowing mercury cell.

Steel gas tank

Wire carrying electricity

Magnesium rod usually placed near the surface for ease of replacement

RUST PREVENTION
Underground steel tanks can rust (pp. 40-41), and replacing them is costly. They are protected from corrosion using an electrochemical reaction. This is known as cathodic protection. A magnesium rod is connected to the steel using copper wire, a good conductor of electricity that will not corrode. Magnesium is more reactive than steel (pp. 24-25), and corrodes instead.

PURIFYING COPPER
Copper is obtained mostly from copper pyrites, a copper ore containing iron and sulfur. The ore is crushed and added to frothy, oily water to remove stones. It is then dried and roasted to remove iron. Further heating with air converts the copper sulfide to copper which is poured into molds and purified by electrolysis. This experiment in a beaker shows the principles of that process of purification.

1 CONNECTING TO ELECTRICITY
The impure copper strip is connected to the positive electricity supply. It becomes the anode. The pure copper strip is connected to the negative electricity supply. It is the cathode. The beaker is filled with electrolyte – copper sulfate solution. Electricity is carried through the solution by ions.

Negative electrode (cathode)

Positive electrode (anode)

Current-carrying wire

Negative electrode (cathode)

Positive electrode (anode) of impure copper dissolves

2 PURIFIED METAL
When the electricity is turned on, a current flows through the electrolyte. At the anode, impure copper dissolves to form copper ions, and the anode gets thinner. Copper ions move to the cathode and are converted to the metal, so copper is deposited on the pure copper strip, making it thicker. The impurities from the anode form a sludge. This sludge is also valuable because it contains tiny amounts of silver and gold which can be extracted.

Copper sulfate solution (the electrolyte)

Pure copper deposited on cathode

Impurities from the copper anode

The chemistry of carbon

CARBON IS A REMARKABLE ELEMENT. It exists as the element in two very different forms: soft black graphite and sparkling diamond (pp. 26-27). It also forms a vast number of compounds. Organic chemistry was originally a term for the study of compounds found only in living things; now it is more widely seen as the chemistry of carbon compounds, except for a few simple compounds such as carbon dioxide and the carbonates, which nclude marble and limestone. For a long time, it was believed that such compounds had some hidden "vital force," and so the chemist could not make them without the aid of a plant or animal. This vital force theory received a blow in 1828 when Friedrich Wöhler (1800-1882) obtained urea, a known organic compound, by heating ammonia with cyanate, usually considered an inorganic compound of carbon. As he had prepared cyanate from animal horn, an organic material, a question mark remained about his findings.

THE ORGANIC CHEMIST
Marcellin Berthelot (1827-1907) prepared many organic compounds from inorganic compounds or elements. He demonstrated that plants and animals are not unique as the only sources of organic compounds. His work in this field finally disproved the vital force theory.

SYNTHESIZING APPARATUS
Berthelot systematically produced many organic compounds. Acetylene is a simple carbon compound (C_2H_2) – a colorless, inflammable gas. In 1866 Berthelot prepared acetylene from its elements hydrogen and carbon. He then passed it through this red-hot glass tube and prepared benzene (C_6H_6), another organic compound.

Glass tube in which acetylene was heated

Berthelot's illustration of the synthesis of benzene

Thistle funnel to trap gases

Unburned carbon forms soot particles

Burning candle wax

WHAT MAKES AN ORGANIC COMPOUND?
This experiment demonstrates that organic compounds (in this case, candle wax) contain carbon and hydrogen. The candle is lit, and the carbon dioxide and hydrogen gases produced from the burning wax are collected. Hydrogen is converted to water vapor, which is trapped by a solid drying agent. The presence of carbon is shown using calcium hydroxide in solution (limewater), the standard test for carbon dioxide.

Cover open to reveal tube

Eyepiece

Sugar solution placed in tube

TWO FORMS OF LACTIC ACID
In 1874 J.H. van't Hoff (1852-1911) realized that optical activity (see right) could be explained only if the four atoms attached to a carbon atom were arranged at the four corners of a pyramid around the central carbon atom. This model is one of two illustrating optical activity.

Pyramid shape

Carbon atom

Bond formed by carbon atom

OPTICALLY ACTIVE SUGAR
A carbon atom's ability to bond to four other atoms (or groups of atoms) leads to an unusual property. If these four atoms or groups are all different, they can form two distinct molecules that are mirror images of each other. Although chemically identical, two such compounds behave differently when polarized light (where the light waves are in only one plane) is shone through them. They rotate the light in opposite directions and are said to be optically active. The polarimeter was introduced in 1840 to measure this optical activity. Sugars show this property; polarimeters were used routinely to analyze sugar syrups. After the 1860s, they became valuable tools for collectors of excise duty to determine the strength of sugar solutions for taxation purposes.

Model of optically active lactic acid

Polarimeter

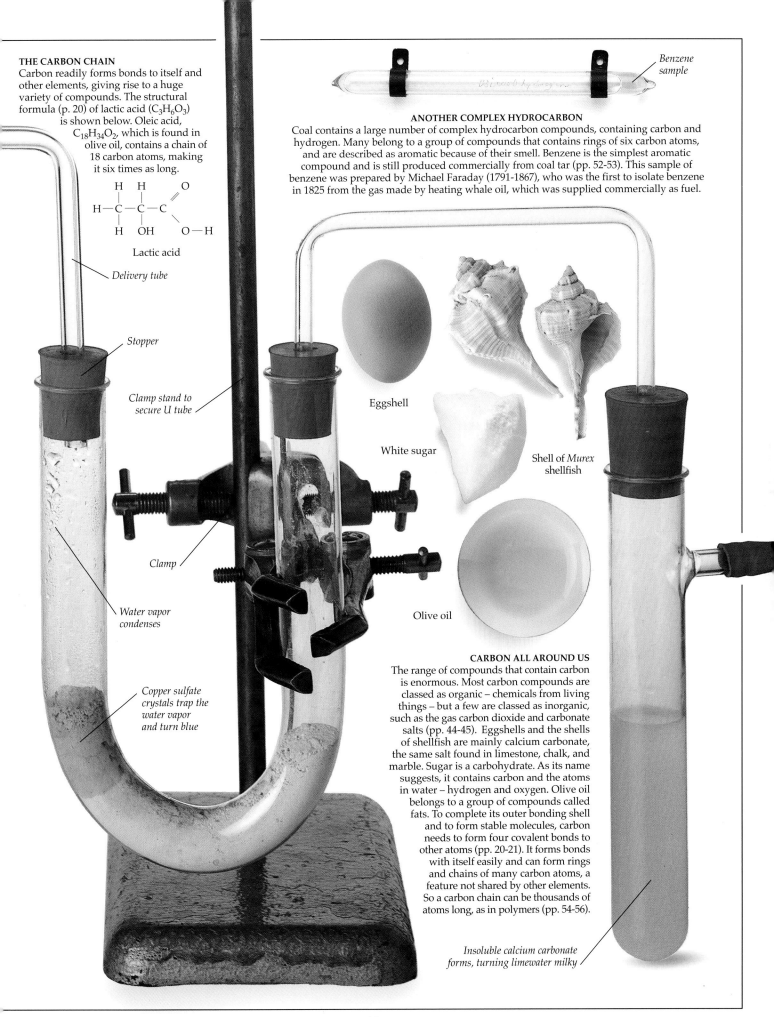

THE CARBON CHAIN
Carbon readily forms bonds to itself and other elements, giving rise to a huge variety of compounds. The structural formula (p. 20) of lactic acid ($C_3H_6O_3$) is shown below. Oleic acid, $C_{18}H_{34}O_2$, which is found in olive oil, contains a chain of 18 carbon atoms, making it six times as long.

Lactic acid

Delivery tube

Stopper

Clamp stand to secure U tube

Clamp

Water vapor condenses

Copper sulfate crystals trap the water vapor and turn blue

Benzene sample

ANOTHER COMPLEX HYDROCARBON
Coal contains a large number of complex hydrocarbon compounds, containing carbon and hydrogen. Many belong to a group of compounds that contains rings of six carbon atoms, and are described as aromatic because of their smell. Benzene is the simplest aromatic compound and is still produced commercially from coal tar (pp. 52-53). This sample of benzene was prepared by Michael Faraday (1791-1867), who was the first to isolate benzene in 1825 from the gas made by heating whale oil, which was supplied commercially as fuel.

Eggshell

White sugar

Shell of *Murex* shellfish

Olive oil

CARBON ALL AROUND US
The range of compounds that contain carbon is enormous. Most carbon compounds are classed as organic – chemicals from living things – but a few are classed as inorganic, such as the gas carbon dioxide and carbonate salts (pp. 44-45). Eggshells and the shells of shellfish are mainly calcium carbonate, the same salt found in limestone, chalk, and marble. Sugar is a carbohydrate. As its name suggests, it contains carbon and the atoms in water – hydrogen and oxygen. Olive oil belongs to a group of compounds called fats. To complete its outer bonding shell and to form stable molecules, carbon needs to form four covalent bonds to other atoms (pp. 20-21). It forms bonds with itself easily and can form rings and chains of many carbon atoms, a feature not shared by other elements. So a carbon chain can be thousands of atoms long, as in polymers (pp. 54-56).

Insoluble calcium carbonate forms, turning limewater milky

The chemistry of life

THE CHEMISTRY OF LIVING SYSTEMS is known as biochemistry. Living organisms and the cells that make them up are composed of water (about 70 percent) and carbon compounds, together with traces of metals and other elements (pp. 18-19). Plants and animals need carbon compounds to grow; when they die and decay, their carbon is recycled back to the earth. The lives of cells are programmed by DNA, which behaves rather like a computer program, storing information for specifying the proteins we need. Proteins build our structure (hair and skin); they act as enzymes which provide the catalysts in humans (pp. 36-37); as hormones they regulate growth and metabolism. Metabolism describes the chemical processes in living organisms that break down complex substances into simpler ones, gaining energy from them. This energy is then used by organisms to live, grow, and reproduce.

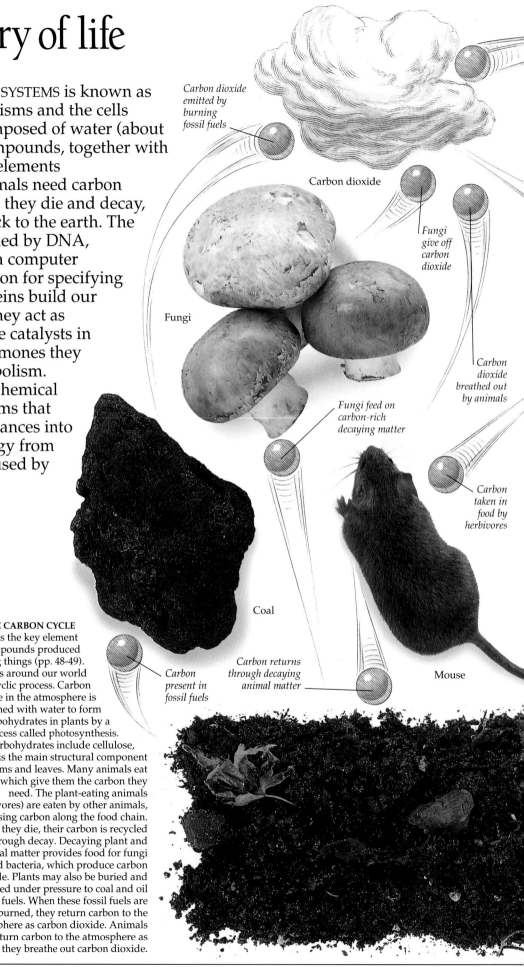

Carbon dioxide emitted by burning fossil fuels

Carbon dioxide

Fungi give off carbon dioxide

Fungi

Carbon dioxide breathed out by animals

Fungi feed on carbon-rich decaying matter

Carbon taken in food by herbivores

Coal

Carbon present in fossil fuels

Carbon returns through decaying animal matter

Mouse

Hans Krebs

GENERATING ENERGY
The biochemist Sir Hans Krebs (1900-1981) arrived in England from Germany in 1933. He proposed a series of reactions to explain how glucose, a sugar, is broken down to yield carbon dioxide, water, and energy. The reactions occur in a cycle; after breaking down one molecule of sugar, the necessary compounds are ready to repeat the process.

THE CARBON CYCLE
Carbon is the key element in compounds produced by living things (pp. 48-49). It moves around our world in a cyclic process. Carbon dioxide in the atmosphere is combined with water to form carbohydrates in plants by a process called photosynthesis. These carbohydrates include cellulose, which is the main structural component of stems and leaves. Many animals eat plants, which give them the carbon they need. The plant-eating animals (herbivores) are eaten by other animals, passing carbon along the food chain. When they die, their carbon is recycled through decay. Decaying plant and animal matter provides food for fungi and bacteria, which produce carbon dioxide. Plants may also be buried and converted under pressure to coal and oil – fossil fuels. When these fossil fuels are burned, they return carbon to the atmosphere as carbon dioxide. Animals too return carbon to the atmosphere as they breathe out carbon dioxide.

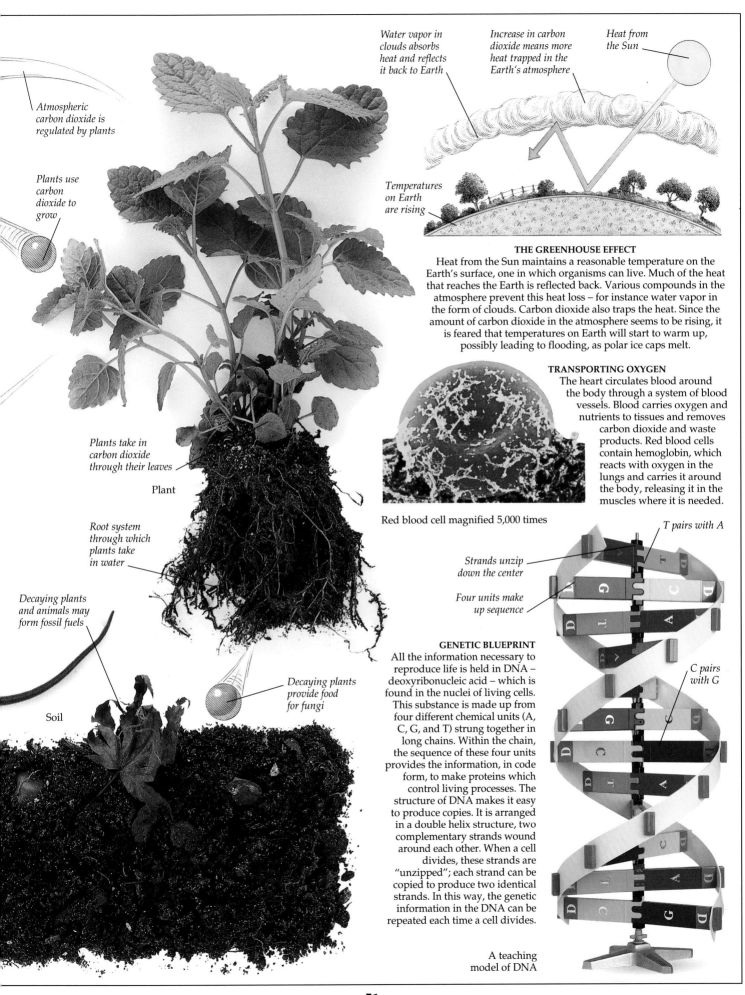

Atmospheric carbon dioxide is regulated by plants

Plants use carbon dioxide to grow

Plants take in carbon dioxide through their leaves

Plant

Root system through which plants take in water

Decaying plants and animals may form fossil fuels

Soil

Decaying plants provide food for fungi

Water vapor in clouds absorbs heat and reflects it back to Earth

Increase in carbon dioxide means more heat trapped in the Earth's atmosphere

Heat from the Sun

Temperatures on Earth are rising

THE GREENHOUSE EFFECT

Heat from the Sun maintains a reasonable temperature on the Earth's surface, one in which organisms can live. Much of the heat that reaches the Earth is reflected back. Various compounds in the atmosphere prevent this heat loss – for instance water vapor in the form of clouds. Carbon dioxide also traps the heat. Since the amount of carbon dioxide in the atmosphere seems to be rising, it is feared that temperatures on Earth will start to warm up, possibly leading to flooding, as polar ice caps melt.

TRANSPORTING OXYGEN

The heart circulates blood around the body through a system of blood vessels. Blood carries oxygen and nutrients to tissues and removes carbon dioxide and waste products. Red blood cells contain hemoglobin, which reacts with oxygen in the lungs and carries it around the body, releasing it in the muscles where it is needed.

Red blood cell magnified 5,000 times

T pairs with A

Strands unzip down the center

Four units make up sequence

C pairs with G

GENETIC BLUEPRINT

All the information necessary to reproduce life is held in DNA – deoxyribonucleic acid – which is found in the nuclei of living cells. This substance is made up from four different chemical units (A, C, G, and T) strung together in long chains. Within the chain, the sequence of these four units provides the information, in code form, to make proteins which control living processes. The structure of DNA makes it easy to produce copies. It is arranged in a double helix structure, two complementary strands wound around each other. When a cell divides, these strands are "unzipped"; each strand can be copied to produce two identical strands. In this way, the genetic information in the DNA can be repeated each time a cell divides.

A teaching model of DNA

Organic synthesis

HEATING COAL IN THE ABSENCE OF AIR GIVES OFF A GAS and a thick tarry substance, to leave coke. Coal gas was produced in large quantities for gas lighting from about 1812. The coal tar residue collected in large amounts, to the embarrassment of the gas industry. During the 1840s, Charles Mansfield (1819-1855) succeeded in fractionally distilling (p. 15) the tar to produce aromatic compounds – so called because of their pleasant smells. The simplest aromatic compound is benzene, and the chemistry of it and the compounds derived from it is called aromatic chemistry. These compounds were initially used as industrial solvents. William Perkin synthesized a dye from one of them – aniline – and opened up a new industry. Other uses for coal tar chemicals rapidly followed. Today most organic chemicals are produced from petroleum and natural gas (pp. 62-63).

WORKING WITH RUBBER
Rubber from the latex of the rubber tree reacts badly to extremes of temperature. Charles Goodyear (1800-1860), an American inventor, simultaneously with Thomas Hancock in England, heated rubber with sulfur and found that this rubber remained flexible over a range of temperatures. He called this process "vulcanization," after the Roman god of fire, Vulcan.

Asphalt

Naphthalene

Anthracene

SYNTHETIC DYES
William Henry Perkin (1838-1907) revolutionized the chemicals industry by making an artificial dye. He was trying to prepare the drug quinine from aniline, a compound derived from coal tar, but he obtained only a dark sticky mess. While cleaning this with alcohol, he found it dissolved to give a dark purple solution, from which he was able to crystallize the dye mauveine. Before this time, dyes had been prepared from vegetable materials such as indigo (pp. 10-11). The new synthetic dye was eagerly bought up by the textiles industry and called "mauve." Perkin went on to synthesize natural smells from chemicals, the beginning of the synthetic perfume industry.

USING ASPHALT
The fractional distillation of coal tar produced a wide number of significant substances that were used to synthesize useful products in the 19th century. Asphalt is the residue from this process, and it is used for covering road surfaces.

Traditional road surface

THE FIRST "MAC"
Thomas Hancock (1786-1865), a rubber manufacturer, and Charles Macintosh (1766-1843), a Scottish chemist, used naphtha from fractional distillation of coal tar to dissolve rubber. This rubber solution was used to produce waterproof cloth for coats that became known as "mackintoshes." One component of naphtha, naphthalene, is used in mothballs. It is a valuable starting point for many synthetic dyestuffs and other materials, such as insect repellents.

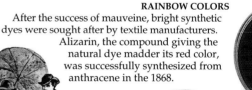

Protection in the rain

RAINBOW COLORS
After the success of mauveine, bright synthetic dyes were sought after by textile manufacturers. Alizarin, the compound giving the natural dye madder its red color, was successfully synthesized from anthracene in the 1868.

Synthetic red dye

Synthetic dyes tend to be brighter than traditional vegetable dyes

Synthetic green dye

Creosote

Benzene

SOAPLESS DETERGENTS

Soap made from animal fats is a detergent or cleaning agent. It tends to form insoluble scum with hard water (pp. 44-45), so soapless detergents were developed to overcome this problem. Many of these are based on benzene, to which a long hydrocarbon chain, similar to those in soaps, is added. Unlike ordinary soaps, the calcium and magnesium salts of these are soluble, so scum does not form.

Soapless detergent

COMMON PRESERVATIVE

Creosote is a distillation product of coal tar. Its insecticide and disinfecting properties make it useful as a wood preservative.

HIGH EXPLOSIVE

The explosive TNT became widely used in World War I (1914-1918). Toluene obtained from coal tar is here being nitrated by pouring it into concentrated nitric and sulfuric acids to produce trinitrotoluene (TNT). When subjected to a mechanical shock, the atoms in this unstable molecule rearrange themselves to form carbon dioxide, steam, and nitrogen gases, causing a thousandfold increase in volume. This sudden expansion is what produces the destructive shock.

Artificial silk fibers

Carbon disulfide

Aniline

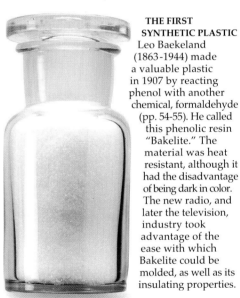

Phenol

THE FIRST SYNTHETIC PLASTIC

Leo Baekeland (1863-1944) made a valuable plastic in 1907 by reacting phenol with another chemical, formaldehyde (pp. 54-55). He called this phenolic resin "Bakelite." The material was heat resistant, although it had the disadvantage of being dark in color. The new radio, and later the television, industry took advantage of the ease with which Bakelite could be molded, as well as its insulating properties.

ARTIFICIAL SILK

Carbon disulfide is a poisonous liquid obtained by heating coke and sulfur in a furnace. It is used as an industrial solvent. In 1892, two British chemists, C.F. Cross and E.J. Bevan, dissolved cellulose in carbon disulfide and alkali, to obtain a viscous solution. Cellulose could be regenerated as fibers by pumping the "viscose" solution through a hole into acid. Originally marketed as artificial silk, these textiles became known as rayon.

THERAPEUTIC DRUGS

Drugs were derived from natural materials, such as willow bark, for centuries. Perkin was trying to synthesize the anti-malarial drug quinine from aniline when he discovered mauveine and launched the dye industry. By the end of the 19th-century, synthetic painkilling and anti-fever drugs had been made from organic compounds. They were overshadowed in 1899 when the German chemical company Bayer introduced aspirin, or acetylsalicylic acid, which is made from benzene in a complicated process.

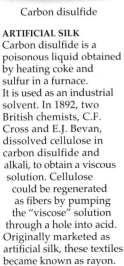

Painkilling drugs

Bakelite television (1950s)

The first plastics

THE FIRST SYNTHETIC PLASTIC was made in the 1860s. Before that, natural materials such as ivory and amber were widely used. Many of these are polymers – from the Greek word *poly*, meaning many, and *mer*, meaning part. Polymers are composed of giant molecules, made up of large numbers of a small molecule strung together in long chains. This small molecule is called a monomer (*mono* means one). The search for synthetic materials started over a hundred years ago to replace materials like ivory, which were becoming scarce, and to make materials that could be molded or extruded as fibers. The first plastics were semi-synthetic polymers and worked by modifying cellulose, the natural polymer in cotton. Later, completely synthetic plastics, such as Bakelite, were made (pp. 52-53).

DECORATED BAG
Synthetic materials resembling ivory were widespread by 1900. They were used for all kinds of products, from knife handles, collars, and cuffs, to this evening handbag. These plastics could be molded when hot into shapes which became rigid after cooling.

THE FIRST PLASTIC
Alexander Parkes (1813-1890) introduced a moldable material made from cellulose nitrate. He dissolved cotton fibers in nitric acid, added a plasticizer such as camphor, and evaporated off the solvent. The material called Parkesine was used to make all kinds of domestic goods like this barrette. Parkes exhibited this first successful plastic in London in 1862.

Molded decorative detail

Clasp

Braided leather strap

Black inlay

Decorative diamante

Silk tassels

HAND MIRROR
This hand mirror is made from ivoride, an ivory substitute. Ivoride, like other plastics, could be easily molded to resemble intricately carved ivory. The early synthetic plastics were modeled to resemble the natural polymers.

CELLULOID EVENING BAG
By 1870, John Wesley Hyatt (1837-1920) was manufacturing celluloid, an ivory substitute, from cellulose nitrate. It was widely used for billiard balls and all kinds of decorative products, such as this evening bag made in 1900.

IMITATION EBONY
This matchbox, dating from 1890, is made of dark-brown ebonite. The plastic is made by vulcanizing rubber.

PLASTIC PEN
When sulfur-containing compounds are heated with rubber, the rubber absorbs them, forming crosslinks between the chains of molecules. Large amounts of sulfur lead to hard, chemically resistant materials, such as the vulcanite used to make this fountain pen.

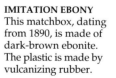

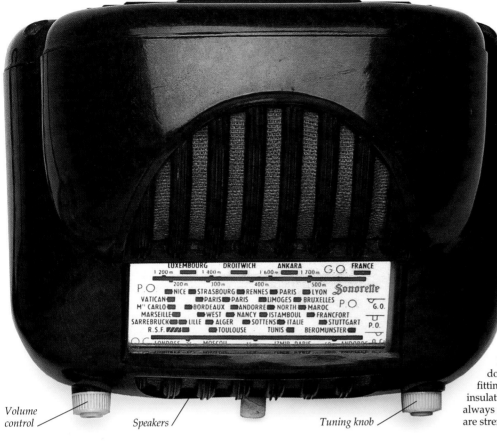

Volume control *Speakers* *Tuning knob*

LEO BAEKELAND (1863-1944)
Belgian-born Baekeland emigrated to the US, where he studied the reaction of phenol and formaldehyde. The dark, tarry mass obtained had previously been ignored by chemists who were interested only in pure crystalline products. In 1907, Baekeland succeeded in controlling a polymerization reaction to produce a synthetic plastic which he called "Bakelite."

BAKELITE RADIO
Bakelite, or phenolic resin, was used for domestic items, such as clocks and electrical fittings. It is resistant to heat and has good insulating properties. The phenolic resins are always dark in color. They are easy to mold and are strengthened using fillers such as textiles.

PLASTIC FILM
Film made of cellulose nitrate was introduced for motion pictures in 1887 and for still pictures in the following year. Cellulose nitrate is notoriously inflammable, so modern film is made from the safer plastic, cellulose triacetate.

CIGARETTE BOX
In the 1920s the search for a light-colored plastic with similar properties to Bakelite, which was always black or reddish-brown, led to the ureaformaldehyde plastics. Using cellulose fillers and suitable coloring materials, both white and colored articles could be manufactured.

SYNTHETIC FIBERS (*below*)
Some plastics can be extruded to form fibers. Textiles used to be derived from natural fibers. Regenerated cellulose from a viscose solution was introduced in 1892 (pp. 52-53). This plastic material could be pumped through fine holes into acid to produce an artificial thread for textiles. Large-scale production was possible with the introduction of a spinning box in 1900. The box collected the filaments without tangling them.

THE PLASTIC AGE
By the 1950s, many different plastics had been developed (pp. 56-57). They were used in industry and throughout the house, especially the kitchen. Strong polyvinyl chloride (PVC) is used as a floor covering. Melamine formaldehyde plastics, which have a good resistance to heat, water, and detergents, were introduced in the mid-1930s. They are laminated by sandwiching alternate layers of plastic and paper or cloth and pressing them to make formica for work surfaces. Other plastics, such as polystyrene, are used for buckets, bowls, and jars. Unfortunately most plastics are not biodegradable; they do not rot away, and they may emit poisonous fumes when burned.

Silk samples from viscose

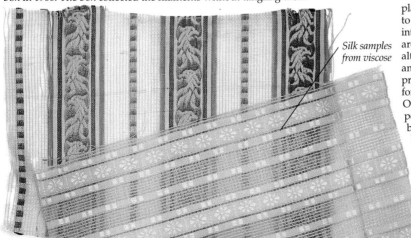

Making synthetic materials

NEW PLASTICS ARE BEING INTRODUCED ALL THE TIME. The first of the thermoplastic materials was polyvinyl chloride (PVC). Observed in the 1870s, it was not successfully produced until the 1930s. Waterproof and weather resistant, it has a wide range of uses: rigid when thick, it makes up guttering, toys, and curtain rails; flexible when thin, it covers electric cables, makes baby pants, and upholstery. Polyacrylic plastics include perspex, a plastic of exceptionally high transparency. Its resistance to shattering makes it invaluable for aircraft canopies. Polythene, or polyethylene, was first discovered in 1933. Like many plastics, it was some time before successful commercial production was achieved in the late 1930s, when its valuable insulating properties were immediately pressed into service for wartime radar equipment. Rigid polyethylene was not produced until the introduction of a catalyst in the 1950s. In the US, the Du Pont company successfully launched nylon-66, which revolutionized the textiles industry. It was strong, stretchy, and nonabsorbent. Today, it is difficult to imagine a world without plastics. Many new processes and products depend upon them.

MAKING NYLON FIBERS
Wallace H. Carothers (1896-1937) joined Du Pont in 1928. He used two chemicals in solutions (an acid and a diamine) to prepare nylon-66. Where the two solutions met, the liquid could be pushed out (extruded) into threads that were stronger than natural fibers. The discovery gave a huge boost to the textile industry and led to a revolution in fabrics.

Nylon drawn out as a thread

MAKING NYLON
Two alternating monomers are used to make nylon-66: adipic acid and hexamethylene diamine. Each has reactive groups of atoms at both ends of a straight molecule – acid groups in the former, and amine in the latter. Each acid group combines with an amine to form long chains of alternating monomers. The diamine is dissolved in water forming the lower layer in the beaker, while the upper layer is a solution of the acid in hexane. Nylon is formed where the two reactants meet and can be pulled out of the beaker and wound around the rod.

Where layers meet, nylon is formed

FASHIONABLE STOCKINGS
Women's stockings made of the new nylon fiber were first marketed in 1940, and nylon soon caught on.

EARLY SAMPLE
This piece of nylon tubing was knitted in 1935 at Du Pont using a slightly different polyamide from the more usual nylon-66. The success of nylon for stockings lies in its strength and its elasticity, which makes it cling rather than wrinkle.

Adipic acid dissolved in hexane

Hexamethylene diamine in water

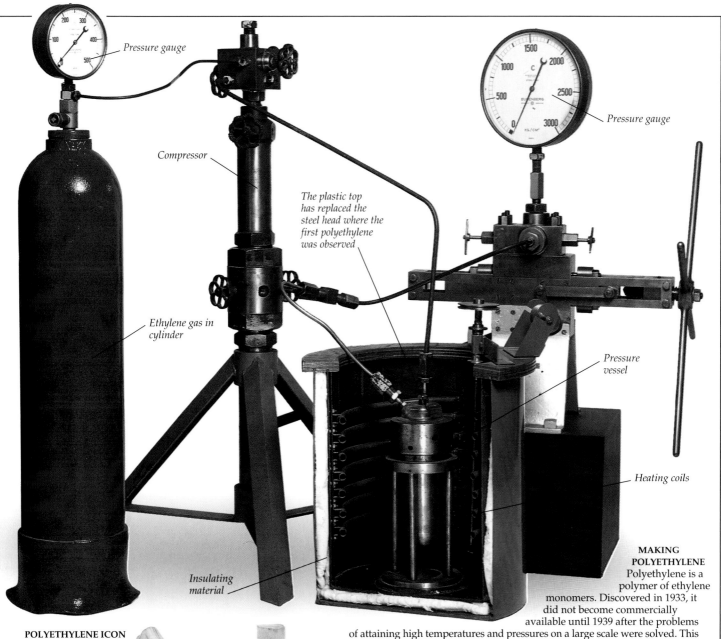

Pressure gauge

Compressor

The plastic top
has replaced the
steel head where the
first polyethylene
was observed

Ethylene gas in
cylinder

Insulating
material

Pressure gauge

Pressure
vessel

Heating coils

MAKING POLYETHYLENE
Polyethylene is a polymer of ethylene monomers. Discovered in 1933, it did not become commercially available until 1939 after the problems of attaining high temperatures and pressures on a large scale were solved. This pressure vessel was used to prepare the first polyethylene samples. While examining the effects of very high pressures on ethylene gas, solid, white particles were observed. Fortuitously, a hole in the equipment had allowed oxygen from air to enter the chamber, which initiated (started) the reaction. This low-density polyethylene is soft, flexible, and clear. In the 1950s a catalyst was introduced, and rigid, high-density polyethylene was obtained.

POLYETHYLENE ICON
This piece of polyethylene is part of the first ton to be manufactured commercially in 1938. Today millions of tons are produced annually for plastic film and molded items.

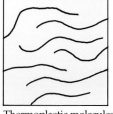

Thermoplastic molecules

Thermosetting molecules

MOLECULAR STRUCTURE OF PLASTIC
All plastics fall into one of two categories depending on how they act when heated. Thermoplastic materials (polyethylene) soften each time they are heated. Thermosetting plastics will not soften again once they have been heated and cooled down (Bakelite). On first heating, these molecules form cross linkages which lead to a permanent rigid structure. They are used to make components such as electric plugs.

Stainless steel shaft

Polyethylene joint

PLASTICS IN SURGERY
Plastics increasingly find applications in replacement surgery, because they do not react with their surroundings. Unlike transplant material from human donors, they do not prompt the body to reject them as foreign material. This hip replacement uses a special ultra-high molecular weight polyethylene.

RECYCLING PLASTICS
This plastic tubing is being made from pellets of polyethylene. Waste polyethylene has been softened with hot water and ground up to produce the pellets. The plastic tubing is blown out using hot air, which shapes and dries the tubing. Recycled plastic is used in the construction industry, where impurities in it are not so important. Only thermoplastics can be recycled in this way.

The story of chemical analysis

FROM EARLY TIMES, assayers (pp. 12-13) tried to analyze basic substances. Chemists often used the senses of smell and taste to detect what things were – sometimes with dreadful consequences. Sir Humphry Davy (pp. 46-47) breathed in all the gases he made – he died young. Johann Glauber (1604-1670) knew that silver forms precipitates with alkalis (pp. 42-43) and carbonates, and he recognized the importance of color in identifying substances. By 1800, the ability of hydrogen sulfide gas to form insoluble salts with certain metals was understood. Karl Fresenius (1818-1897) developed this body of knowledge into a systematic analysis of metals. Other characteristics of substances were also important. When mineral oils began to replace traditional vegetable oils, analytical equipment was developed to measure their volatility.

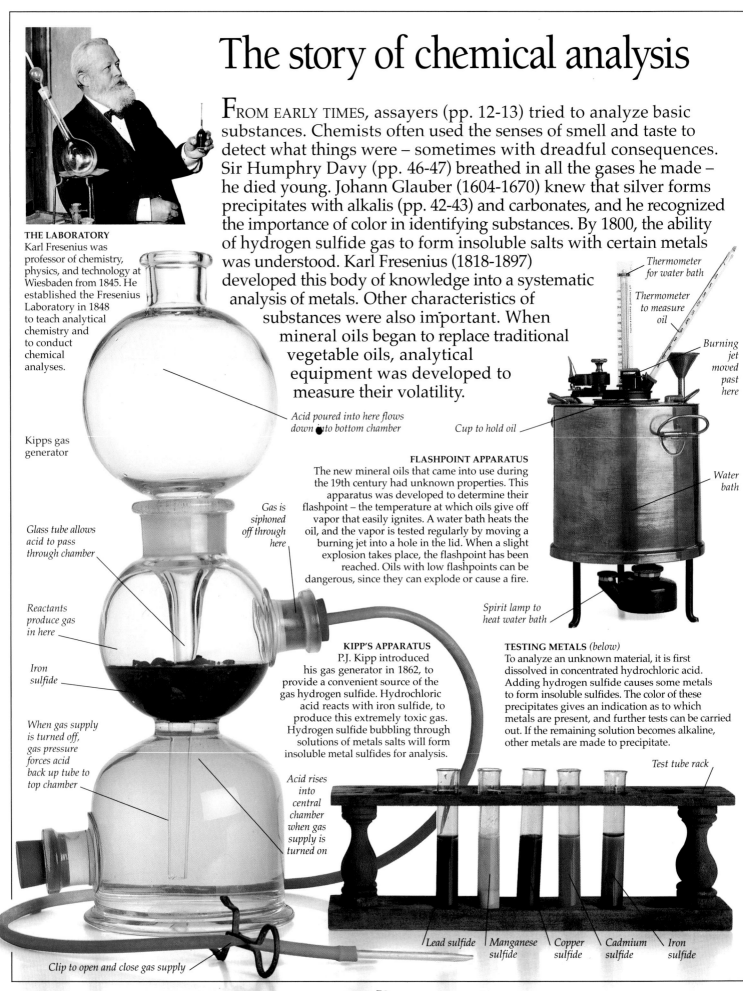

THE LABORATORY
Karl Fresenius was professor of chemistry, physics, and technology at Wiesbaden from 1845. He established the Fresenius Laboratory in 1848 to teach analytical chemistry and to conduct chemical analyses.

Kipps gas generator

Glass tube allows acid to pass through chamber

Reactants produce gas in here

Iron sulfide

When gas supply is turned off, gas pressure forces acid back up tube to top chamber

Acid poured into here flows down into bottom chamber

Gas is siphoned off through here

Clip to open and close gas supply

Acid rises into central chamber when gas supply is turned on

Cup to hold oil

Thermometer for water bath

Thermometer to measure oil

Burning jet moved past here

Water bath

Spirit lamp to heat water bath

FLASHPOINT APPARATUS
The new mineral oils that came into use during the 19th century had unknown properties. This apparatus was developed to determine their flashpoint – the temperature at which oils give off vapor that easily ignites. A water bath heats the oil, and the vapor is tested regularly by moving a burning jet into a hole in the lid. When a slight explosion takes place, the flashpoint has been reached. Oils with low flashpoints can be dangerous, since they can explode or cause a fire.

KIPP'S APPARATUS
P.J. Kipp introduced his gas generator in 1862, to provide a convenient source of the gas hydrogen sulfide. Hydrochloric acid reacts with iron sulfide, to produce this extremely toxic gas. Hydrogen sulfide bubbling through solutions of metals salts will form insoluble metal sulfides for analysis.

TESTING METALS (below)
To analyze an unknown material, it is first dissolved in concentrated hydrochloric acid. Adding hydrogen sulfide causes some metals to form insoluble sulfides. The color of these precipitates gives an indication as to which metals are present, and further tests can be carried out. If the remaining solution becomes alkaline, other metals are made to precipitate.

Test tube rack

Lead sulfide | Manganese sulfide | Copper sulfide | Cadmium sulfide | Iron sulfide

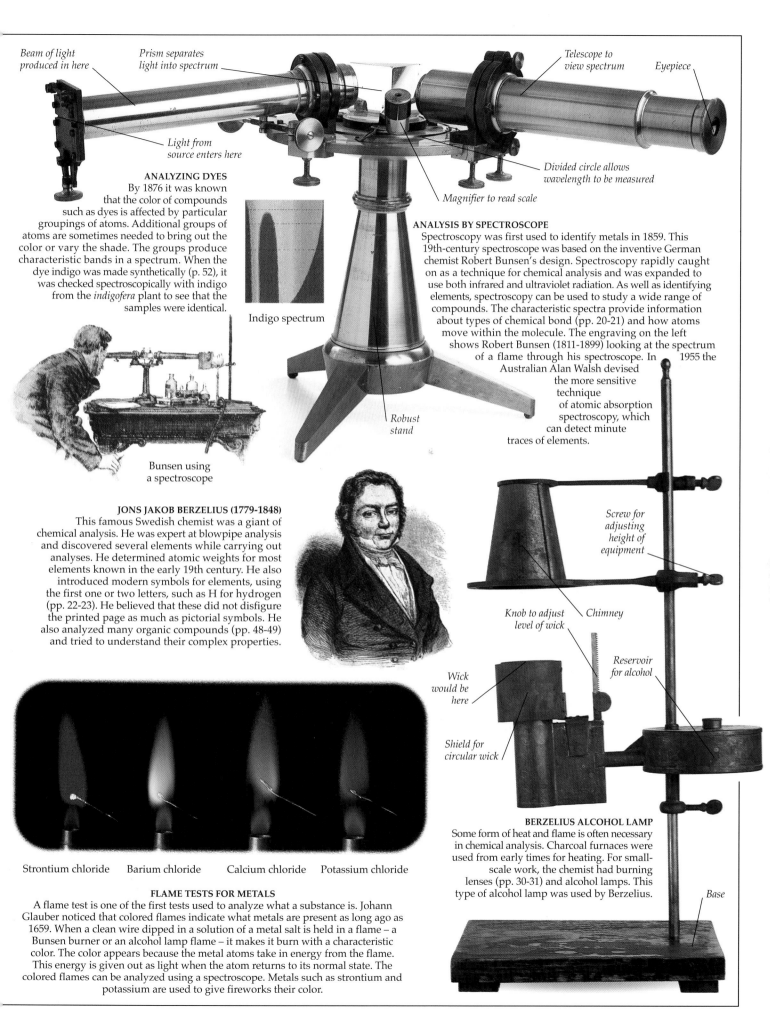

Beam of light produced in here

Prism separates light into spectrum

Telescope to view spectrum

Eyepiece

Light from source enters here

Divided circle allows wavelength to be measured

Magnifier to read scale

ANALYZING DYES

By 1876 it was known that the color of compounds such as dyes is affected by particular groupings of atoms. Additional groups of atoms are sometimes needed to bring out the color or vary the shade. The groups produce characteristic bands in a spectrum. When the dye indigo was made synthetically (p. 52), it was checked spectroscopically with indigo from the *indigofera* plant to see that the samples were identical.

Indigo spectrum

ANALYSIS BY SPECTROSCOPE

Spectroscopy was first used to identify metals in 1859. This 19th-century spectroscope was based on the inventive German chemist Robert Bunsen's design. Spectroscopy rapidly caught on as a technique for chemical analysis and was expanded to use both infrared and ultraviolet radiation. As well as identifying elements, spectroscopy can be used to study a wide range of compounds. The characteristic spectra provide information about types of chemical bond (pp. 20-21) and how atoms move within the molecule. The engraving on the left shows Robert Bunsen (1811-1899) looking at the spectrum of a flame through his spectroscope. In 1955 the Australian Alan Walsh devised the more sensitive technique of atomic absorption spectroscopy, which can detect minute traces of elements.

Bunsen using a spectroscope

Robust stand

Screw for adjusting height of equipment

JONS JAKOB BERZELIUS (1779-1848)

This famous Swedish chemist was a giant of chemical analysis. He was expert at blowpipe analysis and discovered several elements while carrying out analyses. He determined atomic weights for most elements known in the early 19th century. He also introduced modern symbols for elements, using the first one or two letters, such as H for hydrogen (pp. 22-23). He believed that these did not disfigure the printed page as much as pictorial symbols. He also analyzed many organic compounds (pp. 48-49) and tried to understand their complex properties.

Chimney

Knob to adjust level of wick

Reservoir for alcohol

Wick would be here

Shield for circular wick

Strontium chloride   Barium chloride   Calcium chloride   Potassium chloride

BERZELIUS ALCOHOL LAMP

Some form of heat and flame is often necessary in chemical analysis. Charcoal furnaces were used from early times for heating. For small-scale work, the chemist had burning lenses (pp. 30-31) and alcohol lamps. This type of alcohol lamp was used by Berzelius.

Base

FLAME TESTS FOR METALS

A flame test is one of the first tests used to analyze what a substance is. Johann Glauber noticed that colored flames indicate what metals are present as long ago as 1659. When a clean wire dipped in a solution of a metal salt is held in a flame – a Bunsen burner or an alcohol lamp flame – it makes it burn with a characteristic color. The color appears because the metal atoms take in energy from the flame. This energy is given out as light when the atom returns to its normal state. The colored flames can be analyzed using a spectroscope. Metals such as strontium and potassium are used to give fireworks their color.

Monitoring materials

CHEMICAL ANALYSIS IS USED in manufacturing operations to check raw materials and finished products; it can monitor food quality; and medicines are designed, tested, and manufactured with the benefit of chemical analysis. One vital part of analysis is weighing, and accurate balances have been developed since 1800. Some methods of analysis depend on volume measurement – the early studies of gases used a eudiometer (pp. 28-29). For liquids, specialized apparatus such as pipettes and burettes are used. Food analysis assumed great importance during the 19th century; as governments took more responsibility for public health, so chemists were called on to check that foodstuffs were what they were said to be.

ANALYZING COLOR
Mikhail Tswett (1872-1919) studied plant pigments and developed chromatography (pp. 14-15) while trying to extract and separate the pigments.

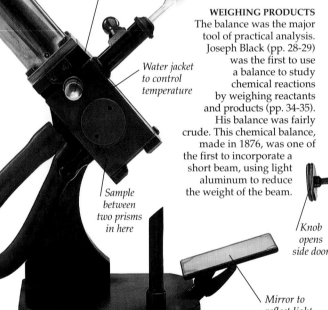

Eyepiece

Screw opens instrument to insert sample

Thermometer

Water jacket to control temperature

Sample between two prisms in here

FOOD ADULTERATION
The first margarine, invented as a butter substitute in 1869, was made from a mixture of beef products (pp. 6-7). Both this and butter were sometimes adulterated by having cheaper vegetable fats added. This could be detected using a butter refractometer. Refractometers were introduced by Ernst Abbe, an optical instrument maker, in 1869. These instruments measure the refractive index of substances – how much light is bent when it passes from air into the substance.

Tube connects water jacket around each prism

Mirror to reflect light through instrument

WEIGHING PRODUCTS
The balance was the major tool of practical analysis. Joseph Black (pp. 28-29) was the first to use a balance to study chemical reactions by weighing reactants and products (pp. 34-35). His balance was fairly crude. This chemical balance, made in 1876, was one of the first to incorporate a short beam, using light aluminum to reduce the weight of the beam.

Knob opens side door

ANALYZING ORGANIC COMPOUNDS
Joseph Gay-Lussac (1778-1850) and Louis Thenard (1777-1857) introduced this apparatus in 1811 to measure the amounts of carbon and hydrogen in organic compounds, such as sugars and starches, by burning them to form carbon dioxide and water. They used an oxidizing agent to make sure the compound burned completely. The carbon dioxide was absorbed and the water vapor was collected and measured. They confirmed that sugars and starches contained hydrogen and oxygen in the same proportions as in water, leading to the name "carbohydrates."

Rider carries small weights for final adjustments

Pans are suspended on knife edges

Pan

Knob lifts pans

F. Sartorius, PA

Balance made by F. Sartorius

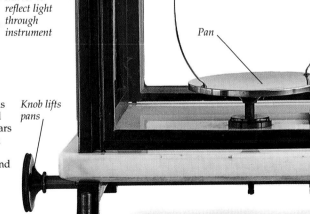

ANALYZING LIQUIDS

The hydrometer has been used since the 17th century to measure the amount of alcohol in liquor. An essential tool of the brewer, it measures the specific gravity of a liquid – its weight compared with that of the same volume of water. This type of hydrometer, designed by Bartholomew Sikes, was used from 1816 to levy excise duty on alcoholic liquids. The "proof" strength is found by looking up tables which take account of the temperature of the liquid.

Analyzing the quality of liquor

Circular weight slots on to the stem

Stem

Eyepiece views both samples at the same time

VOLUMETRIC ANALYSIS

This burette was used in the 19th century to measure the amount of a solution needed to complete a chemical reaction. The flow of liquid is controlled by placing a thumb on the side arm. By lifting the thumb slightly, the liquid can be poured slowly into a flask containing the second solution. The liquid is added until the reaction is complete: in acid-base experiments (pp. 42-43) this may be shown using an indicator that changes color.

Side arm

Hydrometer is suspended in the liquid and the reading on the stem is noted

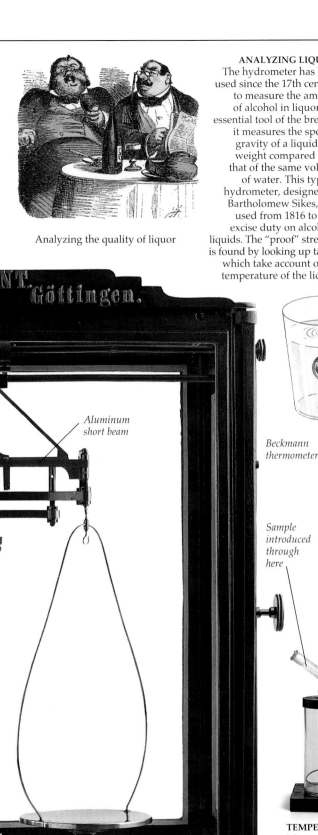

Gőttingen.

Aluminum short beam

Beckmann thermometer

Sample introduced through here

Stirrer

Cooling jacket

Glass rod

Glass rod

Standard solution

Sample solution

White background

Pan stop for pans to rest on when not in use

Leveling screw

TEMPERATURE CHANGE

Measurement of the physical properties of compounds uses apparatus like this. Ernst Beckmann (1853-1923) developed this thermometer to measure the lowering of the melting point for a known weight of a dissolved substance. The thermometer can measure extremely small temperature changes. The scale has gradations of $1/100$ ° C.

KLETT COLORIMETER

The colorimeter was developed during the 19th century to quantify observations based on the depth of color in solution. Industries such as brewing, tanning, dyeing, and printing used colorimetry to check product quality in the early 20th century.

MEDICAL ANALYSIS

The presence of particular compounds in medical samples is vital to medical diagnosis. A variety of ways of analyzing samples – some chemical – can be used. The computer age has changed the look of the chemistry laboratory from a room filled with glass, wooden, and brass apparatus to one that includes blinking screens and high-technological equipment.

The chemical industry

UP TO THE MID-18TH CENTURY, chemical industries were mainly crafts with their roots in ancient times. These included the manufacture of glass, ceramics, soaps, and dyestuffs. In modern times, the most important industrial chemical is sulfuric acid. It is essential for all kinds of industries, from dyestuffs and fertilizers to metallurgy and plastics. Industries such as soap and glass manufacture depend on alkalis, such as potassium and sodium carbonate. Potassium carbonate is obtained from vegetable sources. Nicholas Leblanc (1742-1806) devised a process to produce sodium carbonate from common salt. This process was replaced by the Solvay process, developed in Belgium in 1865. Setting up plants and equipment to make large quantities often causes problems, so for reasons of economy, processes are usually continuous – a supply of reactants are fed in and products are removed continuously, unlike the "batch" process in the laboratory.

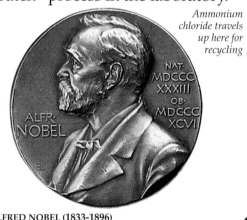

Ammonium chloride travels up here for recycling

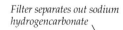
Filter separates out sodium hydrogencarbonate

Ammonia recovery tower

Ammonia is recovered using slaked lime from the kiln

The slaker where lime is slaked with water

CHEMICALS FOR WASHING
Many industries were associated with textiles and clothing. Soaps made by boiling animal fats with alkali have been known since the 12th century. Michel Eugene Chevreul (1786-1889) studied the composition of animal fats. His research led to practical improvements in both the soap and candle-making industries. In major textile-producing areas bleaching was an important industry. In large bleaching fields, textiles were bleached by the combined action of sunlight and lactic acid in buttermilk. Chlorine solutions were used after the late 18th century, but these were unpleasant to produce.

ALFRED NOBEL (1833-1896)
Black gunpowder, invented in China, was the standard military explosive until the 19th century. Nobel was a Swedish inventor who introduced a commercial process for nitrating glycerol and produced nitroglycerine in the relatively safe form of dynamite in 1866. Blasting gelatin was introduced in 1875. Both these explosives were extremely profitable during that era of great industrial expansion, and on his death Nobel left his estate as an endowment for the annual Nobel Prizes.

SODIUM CARBONATE FROM THE SOLVAY PROCESS
The reaction of ammonia, carbon dioxide, and brine (concentrated salt solution) to produce sodium carbonate (soda ash) was studied in 1811, but it was not until 1865 that Ernest Solvay (1838-1922) succeeded in developing a commercial process. In a carbonating tower, brine containing ammonia is saturated with carbon dioxide gas. The resulting sodium hydrogencarbonate is filtered off and heated to give off sodium carbonate and some carbon dioxide, which is recycled. Additional carbon dioxide is obtained by heating limestone (calcium carbonate) in a kiln. Lime, the other product obtained from the kiln, is "slaked" with water and used to regenerate the ammonia, which is the most expensive reactant. The efficient recovery of ammonia is crucial to the commercial success of the process.

Sulfur dioxide (SO₂)
in contact with a
catalyst
forms the trioxide

Sulfur trioxide
(SO₃) reacts with
water to produce
sulfuric acid

Sulfur (S) is burned
in air

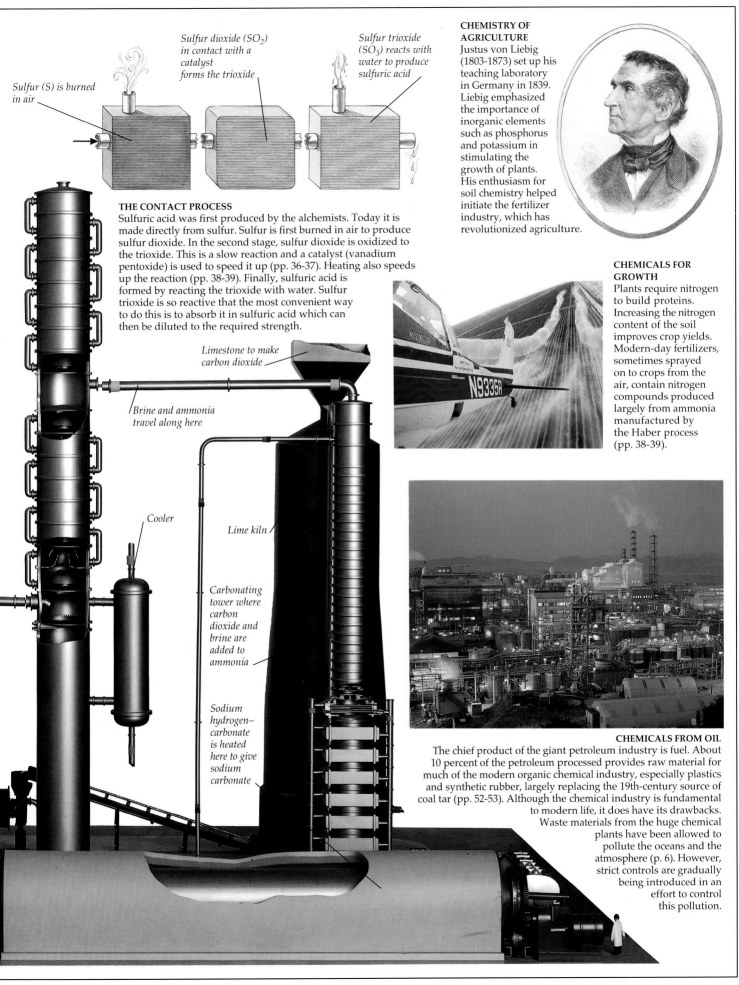

CHEMISTRY OF AGRICULTURE

Justus von Liebig (1803-1873) set up his teaching laboratory in Germany in 1839. Liebig emphasized the importance of inorganic elements such as phosphorus and potassium in stimulating the growth of plants. His enthusiasm for soil chemistry helped initiate the fertilizer industry, which has revolutionized agriculture.

THE CONTACT PROCESS

Sulfuric acid was first produced by the alchemists. Today it is made directly from sulfur. Sulfur is first burned in air to produce sulfur dioxide. In the second stage, sulfur dioxide is oxidized to the trioxide. This is a slow reaction and a catalyst (vanadium pentoxide) is used to speed it up (pp. 36-37). Heating also speeds up the reaction (pp. 38-39). Finally, sulfuric acid is formed by reacting the trioxide with water. Sulfur trioxide is so reactive that the most convenient way to do this is to absorb it in sulfuric acid which can then be diluted to the required strength.

Limestone to make
carbon dioxide

Brine and ammonia
travel along here

Cooler

Lime kiln

Carbonating
tower where
carbon
dioxide and
brine are
added to
ammonia

Sodium
hydrogen–
carbonate
is heated
here to give
sodium
carbonate

CHEMICALS FOR GROWTH

Plants require nitrogen to build proteins. Increasing the nitrogen content of the soil improves crop yields. Modern-day fertilizers, sometimes sprayed on to crops from the air, contain nitrogen compounds produced largely from ammonia manufactured by the Haber process (pp. 38-39).

CHEMICALS FROM OIL

The chief product of the giant petroleum industry is fuel. About 10 percent of the petroleum processed provides raw material for much of the modern organic chemical industry, especially plastics and synthetic rubber, largely replacing the 19th-century source of coal tar (pp. 52-53). Although the chemical industry is fundamental to modern life, it does have its drawbacks. Waste materials from the huge chemical plants have been allowed to pollute the oceans and the atmosphere (p. 6). However, strict controls are gradually being introduced in an effort to control this pollution.

Did you know?

AMAZING FACTS

Skunk spray is made of sulfur compounds known as thiols. (Sulfur is also what gives rotting eggs and onions their unappealing odors.) The human nose can detect the foul smell of skunk-spray thiols in even the smallest concentration of ten parts per billion.

Skunk

What kind of ice never melts? Dry ice is frozen carbon dioxide, the same gas we exhale when we breathe. It is much denser and colder than ice made from water, with a temperature of -109.3°F (-78.5 C). When dry ice is exposed to the air, it sublimates, bypassing the liquid form and going directly from a solid to a gas. The eerie fog dry ice creates is often used in scary movies and theatrical productions.

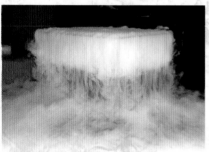

Dry ice

Cyanoacrylate, commonly known as superglue, is a chemical compound that is very useful for sticking things together, but it also helps connect criminals to a crime scene. Forensic chemists use cyanoacrylate fuming to reveal fingerprints on glass and other nonporous surfaces. When crime-scene evidence is held over heated superglue and water, the gas formed by the glue, heat, and moisture reacts with chemicals in the fingerprint, leaving a white deposit behind.

Most of an atom is empty space. More than 99.9 percent of its mass is located in the dense nucleus.

When an object feels hot, the molecules inside it are moving around quickly, in random directions. When an object feels cold, its molecules are moving slowly. The Kelvin scale of temperature is directly related to the speed atoms are traveling. At zero degrees kelvin, or absolute zero (–459°F / 273°C), the molecules stop moving and are as cold as they can be. In the coldest place in the universe—the depths of outer space—the temperature is a few degrees above Absolute Zero.

The world's bitterest known substance, denatonium benzoate, has a use that saves lives. A tiny amount is added to substances such as household cleaners, toilitries, pesticides, and gasoline, giving them a horrible taste that helps prevent curious children or pets from drinking these potentially harmful substances.

Aerogel is the world's lightest (least dense) solid. It is made of silicon, has a porous, spongelike structure, and is mostly air—99 percent of its volume is empty space. According to NASA, aerogel is 1,000 times less dense than glass yet 39 times more insulating than the best fiberglass insulation. A block of aerogel the size of a human being weighs less than one pound, yet can support an object weighing half a ton. NASA has used aerogel on space missions to capture particles from a comet.

The catnip plant, a member of the mint family, contains a chemical compound called nepetalactone. When domestic (or wild) cats inhale its scent, they respond to the nepetalactone by rubbing themselves against the plant, rolling over on it, brushing their cheeks and chins against it, and displaying other playful behaviors. After a few minutes, the cat becomes acclimated to the nepetalactone and leaves. It takes a couple of hours for the cat to "reset" its chemical receptors, and react to catnip again.

Catnip plant

Cat with catnip-filled toy

There is no device to measure how smelly a chemical is, but most chemists would rate ethyl mercaptan among the smelliest compounds. A tiny amount of this compound is added to propane and natural gas supplies (which are odorless), so that people can smell and detect gas leaks. If its vapor is inhaled in large amounts, it can kill humans.

The element Francium is so rare that at any given moment the earth's crust may contain fewer than 30 grams. This radioactive metal has never been isolated in visible amounts, and an amount of Francium sufficient to weigh has never been produced.

Aerogel

Many people find the scent of a brand new car intoxicating. But there is evidence that "new car smell" may actually be toxic. The smell itself comes from a mixture of volatile organic compounds (VOCs), used as adhesives and sealants holding the solid surfaces of the new vehicle together, as well as from the various vinyls, plastics and textiles inside the car. Although studies on health risks caused by "new car smell" are still ongoing, researchers have found that it can cause headaches, nausea, and drowsiness, all of which can contribute to car accidents.

Old newspapers turn yellow as they age because of lignin, a dark-colored polymer that makes wood stiff. At the paper mill, the wood used to make newspaper is pulped, lignin and all. As a newspaper is exposed to oxygen in the air, the lignin molecules begin to change. They absorb light so the paper darkens in color. It only takes a few hours of sunlight and oxygen to start this yellowing process.

Nitroglycerine is a dense, oily liquid that explodes at extremely high temperatures, or if subjected to a physical shock. It is used to make dynamite, but it is also used as a heart medication. The substance (swallowed in tablets or injected in solution) changes into nitric oxide in the body, which widens blood vessels to decrease blood pressure and help alleviate chest pain.

Dynamite

QUESTIONS AND ANSWERS

Q What is a chemical? How do scientists define it?

A Chemistry is the study of matter and its interactions with other matter. So anything made of matter—any liquid, solid, or gas—is therefore a chemical. Any pure substance or mixture of substances is a chemical. But scientists generally use the term "chemical" to refer to a substance that appears homogeneous (the same) throughout its atomic structure.

Q What is the difference between organic chemistry and inorganic chemistry?

A Organic chemistry is the science of the structure, properties, composition, and reactions of organic compounds (compounds that contains carbon). Carbon is only the fourteenth most common element on Earth, yet it creates the largest number of compounds. Inorganic chemistry studies the substances that do not contain carbon and that are therefore not organic. Minerals found in the Earth's crust are an example of inorganic substances.

Q What is analytical chemistry? What do analytical chemists do?

A In the field of chemistry known as analytical chemistry, scientists seek ever-improved means of measuring the chemical composition of natural and artificial material. The techniques of this science are used to identify the substances that are present in a given material, and to determine in what amount they are present. Analytical chemists make important contributions to many fields. In medicine, they set up clinical laboratory tests which help physicians diagnose diseases. In industry, they test raw materials and assure the quality of finished products, from paints to pharmaceuticals. The nutritional values of food you see on food packaging are also determined by an analytical chemist.

Q What is biochemistry? What do biochemists study?

A Biochemistry is the study of the chemicals, reactions, and interactions that take place inside living organisms. Among the subjects a biochemist studies are the chemical regulation of metabolism, the properties of biological entities such as blood cells, and the chemistry of vitamins and minerals.

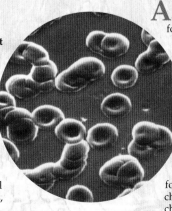
Micrograph of red blood cells

Q What is green chemistry?

A Green chemistry is the use of chemistry to prevent pollution. More specifically, it is the design of chemical products and processes that cut down or eliminate the use and generation of hazardous substances.

Q Is green chemistry the same as environmental science?

A No—although both areas of study seek to make the world a cleaner place, environmental scientists identify sources and solve problems in the Earth's environment, while green chemists seek to solve these problems by targeting pollution prevention at its source, during the design stage of a chemical product or process.

Q What are the principles behind green chemistry?

A The 12 groundbreaking principles of green chemistry were originally developed by Paul Anastas and John Warner in the year 2000. They are: to prevent waste; to design safer chemicals and products; to design less hazardous chemical syntheses; to use renewable feedstocks; to use catalytic reactions to cut down on waste; to avoid chemical derivatives; to maximize atom economy; to use safer solvents and reaction conditions; to increase energy efficiency; to design chemicals and products that biodegrade after use; to analyze in real time to prevent pollution; and to minimize the potential for accidents.

Q What are some of the jobs chemists have?

A Industry is the largest employer of chemists, followed by schools and colleges, and the government. Industrial chemists work in the research or production of polymers, electronics, pharmaceuticals, biotechnology, foods and flavors, detergents, or cosmetics. Government chemists may do research in national laboratories or work in the fields of forensics, environmental chemistry, agricultural chemistry, medicinal research, patent law, or technical writing.

Students explore science in a chemistry class

Q What kinds of classes should I take in school to help me prepare for a career in chemistry?

A Chemists need excellent problem solving and critical thinking skills, and that is what you should focus on. Algebra is particularly useful, as are geometry and trigonometry. Physics and chemistry are closely linked, so you should take courses in both sciences. Chemists also need to be able to communicate clearly and effectively, so if your school offers a technical writing class, sign up for it.

Record Breakers

LIGHTEST ELEMENT
Hydrogen is the lightest element in the universe. It is 14 times lighter than air.

HEAVIEST (MOST DENSE) ELEMENT
Uranium is the heaviest naturally occuring element on Earth.

MOST ABUNDANT ELEMENT IN THE EARTH'S CRUST
Oxygen makes up about 45 percent of the crust. Silicon comes in second at 25 percent.

MOST ABUNDANT ELEMENT ANYWHERE
Hydrogen makes up an incredible 75 percent of all matter in the Universe.

RAREST ELEMENTS
Francium and astatine are the rarest naturally occuring elements on Earth. There are probably less than 30 grams (1 oz) of each of these elements in the Earth's crust.

MOST COMMON ELEMENT IN THE HUMAN BODY
Oxygen (in the form of water) is the most common element in our bodies.

Timeline

Chemistry is known as the science of change—and throughout history, it has brought a great deal of change to our everyday lives. From early people learning to use and control fire to your generation heating up a meal in a microwave oven, chemistry is always around us. Here is a timeline of some of the important people, major developments, and key inventions in the world of chemistry.

Compound microscope

c. 8700 BCE

Copper is in use in early civilizations, primarily for making weapons. Ancient Egyptians make the most of copper's resistance to corrosion by using copper bands and nails in shipbuilding, and copper pipes to carry water.

c. 4000 BCE

The first use of iron by early civilizations in Mesopotamia and Egypt, for spear tips and other weapons. Iron working is introduced to Europe around 1000 BCE.

c. 3000 BCE

Glass is made in Egypt by mixing sand, soda, and lime. Adding metal oxides to the mixture gives color to the glass. The Egyptians are also using bronze, an alloy of tin and copper, at this time.

600 BC

Chinese philosopher Lao-tzu proposes that matter is composed of five elements: water, metal, earth, wood, and fire,—and the forces of yin and yang.

500 BCE

Brass, an alloy of zinc and copper, is in widespread use in ancient Rome.

c. 460 BCE

Birth of Greek philosopher Democritus, who (using the ideas of his teacher, Leucippus) proposes that matter exists in the form of particles, the basis of atomic theory.

c. 450 BCE

The Greek philosopher Empedocles reports that all matter consists of four elements: earth, air, fire, and water. His theory is later supported and developed by Aristotle. This concept also influences the development of alchemy.

Empedocles

c. CE 105

Paper is invented in China by mixing hemp, mulberry bark, and cloth rags with water. European paper-making does not develop until around 1150.

CE 673

"Greek fire," a mix of sulphur, naptha, and lime, is the secret weapon of Roman soldiers. They shoot the liquid through siphons onto enemy ships, which immediately burst into flames.

CE 850

In Spain, the Moors develop a form of copper electroplating, preparing pure copper by reacting its salts with iron.

"Greek fire" is a deadly weapon in a naval battle

1000

The Chinese people develop gunpowder. Gunpowder, a mixture of potassium nitrate with charcoal and sulfur, is used to make fireworks and signal flares, and later, weapons called "fire arrows."

c. 1000–1650

The Age of Alchemy. Alchemists lay the foundations for scientific study as we now know it, particularly chemistry.

1250

Arsenic, a brittle, steel-gray, crystalline metalloid, is discovered by German alchemist Albertus Magnus.

1477

English alchemist Thomas Norton writes about the importance of taste, smell, and color in chemical analysis.

1540

German scientist Valerium Cordus formulates ether as an anesthetic. Ether is made from alcohol and sulfuric acid.

1590

Dutch lensmaker Zacharias Janssen invents the compound microscope (a microscope with more than one lens).

1610

French scientist Jean Beguin publishes the first book dealing only with chemistry.

1620

The term "gas" is coined by Belgian scientist Johannes van Helmont. The word is derived from the Flemish word for "chaos."

1660

Robert Boyle founds the Royal Society of London, a place where groups of scientists hold regular meetings, with a common theme of knowledge by experimental investigation.

1748

American statesman and inventor Benjamin Franklin first uses the term "battery" in relation to charged glass plates.

1755

Scottish chemist Joseph Black is the first person to isolate carbon dioxide in a perfectly pure state.

1774

English scientist Joseph Priestly discovers what he calls "dephlogisticated air." French scientist Antoine Lavoisier will later rename it, oxygen.

1775

Hydrochloric and sulfuric acids are discovered by Joseph Priestly.

1777

Antoine Lavoisier puts forward the idea of chemical compounds, composed of more than one element.

1792

The first society dedicated to chemistry is founded in Philadelphia, Pennsylvania.

1796

British doctor and medical pioneer Edward Jenner creates a vaccine for smallpox. He gives people an inoculation (shot) of the related cow pox virus, so that they could build up immunity to smallpox. Jenner names this process vaccination, after the Latin word for cow, *vacca*.

Edward Jenner vaccinates a child.

1805

French chemist Joseph Louis Gay-Lussac proves that water is made up of two parts hydrogen to one part oxygen by volume.

1808

Modern atomic theory is introduced by British chemist John Dalton. He states that all matter is made of atoms, and that atoms are indivisible and indestructible.

1809

Gas-powered street lighting appears for the first time in London, England.

1827

The phosphorus match is developed by Englishman John Walker. These matches light when struck against any abrasive surface.

1833

English scientist Michael Faraday helps expand knowledge of electrochemistry. He introduces the laws of electrolysis and coins terms such as electrode, anode, cathode, ion, and electrolyte.

Gas lamp

1839

Welsh chemist and inventor William Robert Grove develops the first fuel cell, combining hydrogen and oxygen to produce electrical power.

1848

British inventor and scientist Lord Kelvin develops his temperature scale, which defines zero degrees kelvin as absolute zero, a temperature at which all molecular movement stops.

1850

German chemist Robert Bunsen invents the Bunsen burner. Today, no school science lab is complete without one.

1856

English inventor Henry Bessemer develops the Bessemer converter to produce steel. It is the first process for mass-producing steel inexpensively.

1863

French chemist Louis Pasteur invents the pasteurization process.

1859

The first periodic table of the elements is published by Russian scientist Dmitry Mendeleyev.

1869

Friedrich Mieschler, a Swiss biologist, discovers nuclein, the material now known as DNA (deoxyribonucleic acid).

Bunsen burner

1897

English physicist J. J. Thomson discovers that electrons are negatively charged particles with very low mass. This marks the discovery of subatomic particles, the fundamental building blocks of matter.

1898

Polish-born scientist Marie Curie and her French husband Pierre discover radium and polonium, two radioactive isotopes. Marie and Pierre spent their career studying what Marie called radioactivity.

1909

The pH scale of acidity is devised by Danish chemist Soren Sorensen.

1910

American inventor Thomas Edison perfects the alkaline storage battery. Edison spent eight years and a reported one million dollars perfecting his battery.

1911

Marie Curie becomes the first person to win two Nobel Prizes, earning a chemistry prize in addition to her earlier prize in physics.

1951

Scientists are able to observe single atoms for the first time, using a field ion microscope introduced by Dr. Erwin Mueller.

1951

British scientist Rosalind Franklin discovers the shape of DNA. A number of scientific teams are working on DNA at the same time, but Franklin's extraordinary X-ray photographs of DNA help scientists understand its double-helix shape.

1961

Heat-resistant superpolymers introduced; silicon chips are developed at the same time.

1962

American writer Rachel Carson publishes *Silent Spring*, exposing the hazards of the pesticide DDT, thus challenging people's faith in technology and awakening them to its effect on the environment.

1970

Polish born scientist Roald Hoffman devises the rules which determine the probable locations of electrons around the nucleus.

1985

The launch of the human genome project by the U.S. Department of Energy. Its stated goal is to identify all the genes in human DNA.

1986

The first clinical trial of a synthetic skin named Integra, used to provide grafts for burn victims

1987

A Japanese company develops a plastic with "memory." At low temperatures it can be twisted and shaped, but when it is heated it returns to its original shape.

1996

Dolly, a female sheep, becomes the first mammal to be cloned from an adult mammal's cells, in Edinburgh, Scotland.

Dolly

2001

Researchers unveil the sequence of the human genome; it will take many more years of research to understand the functions of all the genes in the sequence.

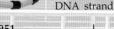

DNA strand

2003

A United Nations treaty known as the Cartagena Protocol aims for more transparency and control in the global trade of GM (genetically modified) crops.

2004

"Green chemistry" is a growing industry, as a reaction to the environmental costs of the chemical revolution. The fundamental idea behind it is that the designer of a chemical is responsible for considering what will happen to the world after the chemical is released.

Find out more

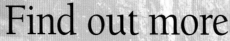

MORE THAN ANY OTHER SCIENCE, chemistry is a part of our everyday lives. From a bowl of cereal in the morning (food manufacturing) to the pillow we sleep on at night (synthetic fabrics), chemistry goes on around us all the time. Here are some ways you can find out more. A visit to a university chemistry laboratory, science museum, or science center will allow you to explore chemistry in action. Perhaps the best way to learn about chemistry is to try a science project, or sign up for a chemistry class or workshop at a science center. Some science centers offer clubs to inspire as well as educate.

TRY A CHEMISTRY EXPERIMENT
You don't have to wait for the science fair to conduct a cool chemistry experiment, such as this erupting "volcano." Look online or at the library for a guide to chemistry projects. You won't need special equipment or chemicals—most projects use materials that are found around the house. As with any scientific experiment, you will need an adult's supervision to ensure your safety.

Molten glass glows with heat.

Tool shapes the base of the vase.

VISIT A GLASSBLOWING STUDIO
As early people learned how to control fire, they began to experiment with chemistry, figuring out how to fuse sand and soda into glass, and how to add oxides to color it. Modern glassblowers often works in the same way early artisans did.

A DAY AT THE MUSEUM
Can you tell the difference between a Bunsen burner and a Bessemer furnace? A visit to a science museum or center will help you figure it out. At a museum, you will see examples of many of the scientific devices found in this book, and find out more about the men and women who were innovators in the field of chemistry. Many science centers are designed so visitors can experiment with chemistry in a fun and exciting way.

KITCHEN CHEMISTRY
Your kitchen is a chemistry laboratory in disguise. Cooking, from baking cookies to making pizza dough with yeast, is chemistry in action. When you cook, try to figure out what principles of chemistry are at work.

USEFUL WEB SITES

www.chemistry.org
Chemistry fun and games for kids from the American Chemical Society

www.chem4kids.com
Chemistry basics made kid-friendly

www.chemmybear.com
A cool chemistry, with projects and games

www.pbskids.org/zoom.games/kitchenchemistry/
Cook up some chemistry in a real or virtual kitchen.

TOUR A CHEMISTRY LAB

Many colleges and universities (and some chemistry-based industries) offer guided tours of their chemistry laboratory facilities to school groups, as part of their community outreach programs. You may be able to see a real working laboratory. In addition, some tours offer the chance to conduct experiments with cool equipment. Ask your science teacher to help you find a program near you, or contact a nearby college directly and ask about upcoming "open" days.

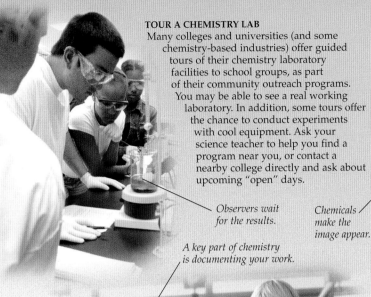

Observers wait for the results.

Chemicals make the image appear.

A key part of chemistry is documenting your work.

CHEMISTRY IN THE DARKROOM

Sign up for a photography workshop, or ask your art teacher if it there are photography classes at school. Learning about the chemistry of photography and printing your own pictures can be fascinating and fun.

TAKE A CHEMISTRY CLASS

If you are interested in chemistry, you can get hands-on experience and explore the wonders of chemistry through a chemistry class at school. You could also sign up for a workshop or chemistry camp. Many science centers and universities offer a variety of courses for young would-be chemists, from one-day sessions to longer workshops. Check the Internet to find a chemistry club or workshop near you.

CHEMISTRY IN A CAVE

The amazing formations you will see if you tour an underground cave (such as this one, in Greece) are a result of chemistry in action. Cave formations, known collectively as speleothems, form when water passes down through the soil above, picking up tiny amounts of limestone as it filters down. As this water drips slowly through the cave's roof, the droplets evaporate, leaving behind tiny amounts of limestone on the cave ceiling and floor. Over millions of years, particle by particle, the speleothems grow.

Places to Visit

OREGON MUSEUM OF SCIENCE AND INDUSTRY, PORTLAND, OR
Hundreds of interactive exhibits, hands-on demonstrations, and science labs

SCIENCE MUSEUM OF MINNESOTA, ST. PAUL, MN
Tons of hands-on fun along with breathtaking views of the Mississippi River

MIAMI MUSEUM OF SCIENCE, MIAMI, FL
This fantastic museum has won national recognition for its education programs.

ST. LOUIS SCIENCE CENTER, ST. LOUIS, MO
More than 700 hands-on exhibits are housed in the permanent collection, with traveling exhibitions rounding out the display.

CENTER OF SCIENCE AND INDUSTRY, COLUMBUS, OH
In its 40-year history, more than 17 million visitors have found out that science can be fun at this innovative museum.

SCIENCE MUSEUM OF VIRGINIA, RICHMOND, VA
Hundreds of permanent hands-on exhibits designed to help visitors delve into the world of chemistry and science

THE SCIENCE PLACE, DALLAS, TX
This is the discovery destination in Dallas, with more than 200 hands-on exhibits and a strong educational program.

FRANKLIN INSTITUTE SCIENCE MUSEUM, PHILADELPHIA, PA
A hands-on science center as well as an archive of artifacts related to scientific achievements

MUSEUM OF SCIENCE AND INDUSTRY, CHICAGO, IL
This museum is jam-packed with excellent exhibits to help you explore science.

MARYLAND SCIENCE CENTER, BALTIMORE, MD
More than half a million visitors a year explore the excellent exhibits at this museum.

Glossary

ACID A hydrogen-rich chemical that reacts with metals to form salts, and with metallic oxides and bases to form a salt and water. Acids have a sour taste, turn litmus paper red, and have pH values of less than 7.

ACID RAIN Precipitation (rain, snow, or fog) containing harmful amounts of nitric and sulfuric acids, formed primarily by nitrogen and sulfur oxides released into the atmosphere when fossil fuels are burned.

ALCHEMY A medieval and Renaissance practice predating modern chemistry, alchemy is the endeavor to find the key to the transformation of chemical substances. The basis to alchemy was the theory that all matter is composed of various combinations of four key elements: air, water, earth, and fire.

ALEMBIC A container used for distillation

Alembic

ALKALINE A description of water or soil that contains a large amount of alkali substances (various soluble salts); in general, refers to anything with a pH above 7. Bases are always alkaline by definition.

ALLOY A mixture containing two or more metals usually fused together, or dissolving into each other when molten

ASSAYER A person who tests, or assays, minerals for their metal content

ATOM The smallest component of an element that can exist alone or in combination. An atom is composed of an electron cloud and a central nucleus.

BASE Any of the various water-soluble compounds that turn litmus paper blue, react with an acid to form salt and water, and have a pH of 7 to 14.

BIOCHEMISTRY The science that studies the chemistry of living organisms, including human beings

BOND The force that holds atoms together in a molecule. When two atoms share electrons, or when one atom lends one ore more electrons to another, the atoms are joined in a chemical bond.

BUNSEN BURNER A gas burner used in laboratories. Bunsen burners have an air valve to regulate the mixture of gas and air.

CARBON CYCLE The continuous exchange by which carbon moves through the biosphere; the processing of carbon dioxide into carbohydrates by photosynthesis, and its return to the atmosphere by animal metabolism and decomposition

CATALYST A substance that increases the rate of a chemical reaction without being consumed in the reaction

CHEMICAL An element (for example, chlorine) or a compound (for example, sodium bicarbonate) produced by a chemical reaction

CHEMICAL REACTION Any change which alters the chemical properties of a substance or which forms a new substance

CHEMISTRY The science of matter; the branch of the natural sciences dealing with the composition of substances, and their properties and reactions

COMPOUND A substance formed by the chemical union of two or more elements or ingredients in definite proportion by weight

CONDUCTOR Any substance that readily transmits electricity or heat

COVALENT BOND A bond between two atoms formed by the sharing of a pair of electrons

DENSITY The ratio of the mass of a substance to the volume it occupies. If two objects have the same volume, the one made of a denser material will weigh more.

DISTILLATION The process of heating a liquid to its boiling point, condensing the vapors through cooling, and collecting the condensed liquid in a separate container.

DNA (DEOXYRIBONUCLEIC ACID) The molecule responsible for carrying the genetic information necessary for the organization and functioning of most living cells, and for controlling the inheritance of characteristics.

ELECTROLYSIS The process of breaking a chemical compound down into its elements by passing a direct electrical current through it. Electrolysis of water, for example, produces hydrogen and oxygen.

ELEMENT Any of the more than 100 known substances (92 of which occur naturally) that cannot be separated into simpler substances, and that constitute, or make up, all matter.

EMULSION A suspension of droplets of one liquid in another liquid (such as oil in water). The two liquids do not combine but are suspended within one another.

ENZYME A protein that acts as a catalyst, speeding up the rate of a chemical reaction

ESSENTIAL OILS Potent, highly aromatic oils extracted from plants, through distillation, steam, or expression

EXTRACT An infusion; a solution obtained by steeping or soaking a substance, usually in water. Also, a verb meaning to distill.

Helium balloons

HELIUM The second lightest and second most abundant element; a gas atom whose nucleus consists of two protons and two neutrons

INSOLUBLE Refers to a substance that is incapable of being dissolved in a liquid

IONIC BOND A chemical bond between two ions that results from the force of attraction between positive and negative ions

LITMUS A purplish coloring material obtained from lichens (fungi). Litmus is applied to paper to make litmus paper. This paper will turn blue in alkline solutions and red in acidic solutions, providing a rough acid-base indicator.

Strips of litmus paper

MALLEABLE Capable of being shaped by being hammered, pressed, formed, or bent

METAL Any of several chemical elements that are usually shiny solids, can conduct heat or electricity, and can be formed easily into sheets

METALLURGY The science of metals and their extraction from naturally occuring ores, to prepare them for practical use

MOLECULAR STRUCTURE The three-dimensional arrangement of atoms in a molecule

Molecule

MOLECULE A collection of two or more atoms held together by chemical bonds; the smallest unit of a compound that displays the properties of the compound. The name comes from the Latin word *molecula*, meaning a small mass.

NEON A colorless inert gaseous element. Neon lights are made from glass vacuum tubes filled with neon gas at a low pressure.

NEUTRON One of the basic particles which make up an atom. A neutron and proton have about the same weight, but the neutron has no electrical charge.

NOBLE GAS Any of a group of rare gases (helium, xenon, argon, and others) that exhibit great stability and extremely low reaction rates. The noble gases are also called inert gases.

NUCLEUS The dense, positively charged center of an atom

NYLON The first completely synthetic fiber. Nylon is known for its high strength and excellent resillience.

ORGANIC Relating or belonging to the class of chemical compounds containing carbon.

OXIDATION The chemical process of oxygen combining with an element or compound; for example, the oxidation of iron to form rust

PARTICLE A microscopic object with a definite mass and charge

PERIODIC TABLE A chart showing all the elements arranged in columns with similar chemical properties

PH SCALE A scale that is used to measure acidity. The scale ranges from 1 to 14, with 7 being neutral. Numbers lower than 7 indicate acidity; numbers higher than 7 indicate alkalinity.

PLASTIC A generic name for synthetic or semisynthetic materials that can be molded or extruded into objects, films, or filaments, or used to make coatings.

POLYETHYLENE A plastic made from ethylene, used in making trash bags, milk jugs, shampoo bottles, and cable coating, among other things

PROTEIN A large molecule composed of one or more chains of amino acids in a specific order. Proteins are required for the structure, function, and regulation of cells, tissues, and organs.

The glow of neon lights the night.

PROTON One of the basic particles that makes up an atom. The proton is found in the nucleus and has a positive electrical charge equal to the negative charge of an electron. The proton also has a mass similar to that of a neutron.

REACTIVE Tending to react quickly or vigorously, or unstable when exposed to shock or heat

REDUCTION Any process in which electrons are added to an atom or ion

RUST A red or brown, brittle oxide coating that forms on iron or its alloys. Rust forms as a result of exposure to air and humidity, or to various chemicals.

SALTS Compounds that can be formed by replacing one or more of the hydrogen ions of an acid with another positive ion

Salt derived from copper

SOLUBLE Capable of being dissolved in another substance

SOLUTION A homogeneous mixture of two or more substances; often (but not always) a liquid

SPECTROSCOPE A scientific instrument that breaks light into its component wavelengths for measurement

SUSPENSION A mixture in which fine particles are suspended in a fluid

SYNTHESIS The process of putting parts together to form a new whole; in chemistry, the process of forming compounds out of simpler elements

UNREACTIVE Not showing signs of a chemical reaction

VAPOR A suspension of particles of a certain substance in the air

VOLTAIC PILE A simple battery consisting of cells arranged in a series. The voltaic pile was devised by Italian inventor Alessandro Volta.

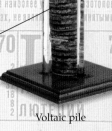

Layers of cardboard rest between disks of copper and zinc.

Voltaic pile

Index

Acknowledgments

The publisher would like to thank:
John Becklake, Chris Berridge, Roger Bridgman, Stewart Emmens, Stephen Fougler, Graeme Fyffe, Ian Carter and Science Museum Library Staff, Brian Gilliam and object handling team, Derek Hudson, Douglas Millard, Sue Mossman, Derek Robinson, Robert Sharp, Peter Stephens, Kenneth Waterman, and Anthony Wilson for advice and help with the provision of objects for photography at the Science Museum; Frances Halpin for technical advice and help with the laboratory experiments; Evelyn Richards, laboratory technician at Harris CTC, London; Deborah Rhodes for page make-up; Neil Ardley for advice in the early stages; Susanne Haines for the calligraphy on pages 22-23; Karl Adamson, Dave King and Colin Keates for photography; Parker Pen UK Ltd for the pen on page 46; Johnson Mathey for the catalytic converter; Boots Co. for the water softener; Ed Evans at the Coal Research Establishment, British Coal Corporation for technical advice.

DTP Manager Joanna Figg-Latham
Illustrations John Woodcock
Index Jane Parker

Picture credits
t=top b=bottom c=center l=left r=right

Brown Brothers 41tl. Dupont Co, New York 56tl. Mary Evans Picture Library 10tl; 15bl; 19cr; 25tl; 26br; 34cr; 52bl; 53tr; 59cl. Werner Foreman Archive 11br. Hulton Deutsche Picture Collection 22tl; /Bettmann Archive 52tl; /Bettmann Archive 55tr. Robert Harding Picture Library 33cl; 41bl. Hutchinson Picture Library 18cr. Mansell collection 35br; 40bl; 46c; 59c; 62cl. NASA 35tl. Robert Opie Collection 7tr; 56cr. Ann Ronan at Image Select 11tr; 30bl; 30tr. Royal Institution /Godfrey Argent 20cr; 21tr. Science Museum Photo Library 7cr; 26c; 28tl; 31tl; 40tl; 55br; 60 bl.

Science Photo Library /Simon Fraser 6bl; /David Campline 9tl; /CNRI 9ct; /Dr Mitsuo Outsuki 17br; /Professor Stewart Lowther 27cl; /William Ramsay 32cr; /Philippe Pailly 33tr; 34tl; /McGrath Photography 38tl; 39tl; James Holmes 46br; 50bl; 51cr; /James Holmes 57br; /Hank Morgan 61br; 63cr; /Simon Fraser 63br. Ullstein Bilderdienst 39tr; 58tl.

Alamy: Robert E. Barber 64tl; imagebroker 64cl. AP Wideworld: 69tl.
Bridgeman Art Library: Byzantine/Prado, Madrid, Spain 66c
Corbis: Lester V. Bergman 65bl; Bettmann 67tl; Jim Cummins 65tr; Macduff Everton 68c; Najlah Feanny 67cr; Gail Mooney 69br; Romane P. 69cl. DK: Judith Miller Hamptons 66tr; Clive Streeter Courtesy of The Science Museum, London 70cl
Getty Images: Stone 69tr

NASA Marshall Space Flight Center: 64tr
Science Photo Library/Photo Researchers: 66br; 68br

Jacket images: *Front:* Corbis: (tr). DK Images: Clive Streeter/The Science Museum, London (ca, tcl). Getty Images: The Image Bank (tcr). *Back:* DK Images: Clive Streeter/Calligraphy by Susanne Haines (cal); Clive Streeter/The Science Museum, London (bcl, bl, car).

With the exception of the items listed above, and the objects on pages 1, 2c, 2bl, 3c, 5, 6, 8-9, 12b,14b, 15, 16-17b, 17r, 18bl, 20, 21c, 25b, 28-29b, 30l, 33tr, 33c, 34b, 35c, 36-37c, 37, 38-39b, 41r, 42-43, 44b, 45r, 45c, 46r, 47c, 48-49c, 50-51c, 52c, 53t, 53c, 53br, 56e, 58bl, all the photographs in this book are of objects in the collections of the Science Museum, London.